On Fraternity

On Fraternity
Politics beyond liberty and equality

Danny Kruger

Civitas: Institute for the Study of Civil Society
London
Registered Charity No. 1085494

First Published April 2007

© The Institute for the Study of Civil Society 2007
77 Great Peter Street
London SW1P 2EZ
Civitas is a registered charity (no. 1085494)
and a company limited by guarantee, registered in
England and Wales (no. 04023541)

email: books@civitas.org.uk

ISBN 978-1-903386-57-6

Independence: The Institute for the Study of Civil Society
(Civitas) is a registered educational charity (No. 1085494)
and a company limited by guarantee (No. 04023541). Civitas
is financed from a variety of private sources to avoid over-
reliance on any single or small group of donors.

All publications are independently refereed. All the Institute's
publications seek to further its objective of promoting the
advancement of learning. The views expressed are those of
the authors, not of the Institute.

Typeset by
Civitas

Printed in Great Britain by
The Cromwell Press
Trowbridge, Wiltshire

Contents

Author

Danny Kruger is special adviser to David Cameron MP, the leader of the Conservative Party. He was formerly chief leader writer at the *Daily Telegraph* and director of studies at the Centre for Policy Studies. He has degrees in modern history from Edinburgh University (M.A., 1997) and Oxford University (D.Phil., 2000).

Author's Acknowledgements

This essay has been quite long in the writing and I have benefited from a lot of help. Tim Evans, Peter Franklin, John Hayes and Tim Montgomerie have been strong if unwitting influences. Douglas Carswell, David G. Green, Daniel Hannan, Steve Hilton, Oliver Letwin, Jesse Norman, Douglas Smith and David Willetts all read and commented on an earlier draft of the essay. David Green kindly hosted a seminar at Civitas to discuss it, and my thanks to David Coleman, David Goodhart, Douglas Murray, Nick Seddon and Justin Shaw for their advice. Any mistakes in what follows are all my own. I should also stress that I do not speak for the Conservative Party.

Introduction

The Wall and the Desert

One sure symptom of an ill-conducted state is the propensity of the people to resort to theories.

Edmund Burke,
Thoughts on the Cause of the Present Discontents, 1770

Cardinal Josef Ratzinger was proclaimed Pope Benedict XVI, in succession to John Paul II, on the Vatican balcony on 19 April 2005. It was the time of the British general election campaign. Moments after the announcement, an email flashed around from some wag in Conservative Campaign Headquarters, echoing the way that constituency results are announced on election night: 'Vatican: Con. gain.'

Benedict is certainly conservative, perhaps even more so than his predecessor. And yet his election signalled an important shift in the expression of papal conservatism — one, I believe, which reflects the shift in political conservatism that is necessary in Britain.

John Paul's main political concern in the 1980s, the time of his vigour, was with the wall which passed through Berlin and divided the free west of Europe from the communist east. His wish was to dismantle the dominating structures of communism, liberating individuals and nations from state oppression. His object was freedom.

Twenty years on, Benedict sees a different problem: not a wall, but a desert. His concern is with the arid emptiness in Western culture, an emptiness which extends from private loneliness all the way to environmental desolation. 'The external deserts are growing', he said in his first papal

1

pronouncement, 'because the internal deserts have become so vast.'[1] His object is fraternity.

In the 1980s the Conservatives, like John Paul, were wall-breakers. They overran the frontiers of the state, tore down the union-imposed restrictions on labour, and with a 'big bang' like the blast of trumpets outside Jericho, demolished the fortresses of the City which protected the capitalists from competition. The entrepreneurial energies of the people were released and wealth grew greatly.

But the 1980s also saw the defoliation of the natural landscape. In *The City of God* Augustine quotes a Briton saying 'the Romans make a desert and they call it peace'. The Tories might be said to have made a desert and called it freedom. Hundreds of local institutions, non-commercial and quasi-commercial, were swept away in the flood of reform. Small high-street grocers and bakers disappeared. Family-run pubs were subsumed into giant chains. Whitehall desolated local government, and turned a blind eye to the steady erosion of the family and civil society by the cult of individual freedom.

This trend—social desertification we might call it—has grown greatly since the Conservatives left office, compounded by a Labour Government which has even less respect for the established and the natural. The emptiness in our culture is apparent in the rates of family breakdown and the prevalence of drug addiction and violent, alcohol-fuelled crime; in the neglect of the old and the precocious sexuality of children; in the cult of vicarious narcissism which is 'reality TV'; in the popular addiction to shopping as a means of self-definition, and in the astronomical scale of private debt which is necessary to maintain the habits of consumerism. It is also apparent, conversely, in the receptive hearing which militant Islam gets from some young Asians in Britain, and in the hostility to Asians among some young whites. In the social landscape benign cultures are shrivelling, and nasty proxies are recrudescent. Only weeds and thistles grow vigorously.

What is the response to this cultural aridity? The danger is that the presence of the desert will prompt a new spate of wall-building. At the 2005 general election, politicians of both main parties appealed to the rhetoric of the fortress. Focus groups told them that people did not seem to want more 'freedom' or 'choice'. They wanted more order and security. So the politicians adopted the mentality of the laager. The Labour Party promised to preserve and extend the state welfare system, the wall which—so they claim— surrounds the poor and protects them from the harsh winds of freedom. And if the Conservatives remained true to the ideal of freedom in the economy and the public services, they also appealed to the native instincts of a fearful and defensive Britain, offering to shore up walls against the European Union and immigrants, against burglars and 'yobs'.

The Conservative offer was right as far as it went. There do need to be walls around the national home and the family home. If, as Shakespeare's John of Gaunt put it, the sea around our island once served 'in the office of a wall', it does so no longer.[2] One of the government's primary duties is to maintain the integrity of our borders, against both mass immigration and foreign rule. Another is to preserve the walls around the Englishman's home, and to help him defend his family from criminals.

And yet more is necessary than this. For between those walls—the one around our island and the one around our homes—is a large space. This is the field of civil society. Here people congregate for all the business and pleasure of life, performing the transactions of love and profit which make the nation grow. These transactions are, or should be, private, mediated where mediation is necessary through independent institutions, constructed and maintained by free people.

****

The purpose of this essay is to explain and celebrate the place of civil society, the voluntary combination of free people, in our politics. We are witnessing, and should welcome, a revival of what I simply call fraternity. It might, less abstractly, be called the culture of belonging, or the sense of community. I call it fraternity because it fits into the famous rhetorical triad of the French revolution, along with liberty and equality; and the three of these compose the ideological architecture of what follows.

Fraternity is on the rise for reasons which are best explained by experts, but apparent to all. As globalisation widens the horizons of our familiar landscape and technology speeds up time, we turn instinctively towards the small and slow. We are searching for rootedness, and for safety. This search need not be—though for many it is—an absolute rejection of the new world, a retreat behind walls; it can simply be a sensible response to the need for a secure base from which to explore the new world, to which to return. Fraternity is not the bunker mentality; it is the yearning for home.

****

In the fourth century BC, Plato asked the question that has occupied political philosophy ever since: what is justice?[3] A few years later, Aristotle asked the same question in a more human way: how shall men live together?[4]

In Britain in 2007 we are asking these questions again. Our society has three stark features which demand attention. The first is a widening gap between rich and poor. The health, even the existence, of a community depends on a degree of shared experience, and this must include some

4

shared experience of the standard of living. Today, standards of living are diverging markedly. And not only is relative poverty—the degree of difference between the classes—getting worse. Social mobility—the ease with which one can rise or fall in wealth according to one's own efforts and abilities—is in decline. Some millions of people find themselves falling behind as the rest of society advances, and unable to change their lot; the consequence, in some hundreds of communities, is endemic debt, depression, drugs, alcoholism, crime, and, cause and effect of all of these, family breakdown.

The second worrying feature of our society is the slow but profound collapse of the relationship between the generations. Stages of life unknown to our ancestors, long periods between childhood and adulthood (the attenuated adolescence which seems to be starting ever earlier and finishing ever later) and between retirement and death, present major social challenges. The vast army of the retired and soon-to-retire are in conflict with our increasingly strident and alienated youth, not only for material resources and political power, but also—just as important—for cultural airtime and national respect. Criminality and boredom at one end of the life cycle, indignity and boredom at the other, testify to the waste of human capital in our current arrangements, and to the burden we unnecessarily place on the harassed middle-aged.

The third feature is the presence of large communities with different national origins and, therefore, alternative cultural traditions. The picture painted by George Orwell of the urban population in World War Two, with 'their mild knobby faces, their bad teeth and gentle manners', was a picture of a people who were, if strong in their local loyalties, culturally homogenous. Today, our cities are peopled from across the globe. Orwell spoke admiringly when he said, of British society, 'the diversity, the chaos of it!' But we have stronger contrasts than that between old ladies on bicycles, and 'the clatter of clogs in the Lancashire mill towns'.[5]

What is justice? How can we live together? The Left have an answer. To resort to the organic metaphor, their approach to the widening divisions between classes, generations and cultures is to lay waste to the landscape, with its peculiar and various habitations of wood and stone, and erect in their place a great steel citadel to house everyone together and equally: the state.

There is an alternative answer: not equality, but fraternity. It is not our common submission to the central state that will help us live together, but our various and overlapping memberships of a far larger and more diverse range of associations. The famous lines of Burke are justly revered by the Right:

> to be attached to the subdivision, to love the little platoon we belong to in society, is the first principle (the germ, as it were) of public affections. It is the first link in the series by which we proceed towards a love to our country and to mankind[6]

Modern critics of conservatism are fond of pointing out that the context of these lines is a call for aristocratic solidarity against the forces of democracy—that the 'little platoon' referred to is not a club, or a village, but a class. But the principle applies generally, as any reading of Burke will show. It is through common interest with and affection for the people closest to us, be they of the same station or the same locality or united on some different principle altogether, that we discover our interest with and affection for people in general.

This is a fact of life which is emphasised by a thinker I draw on heavily in this essay: G.W.F. Hegel. To 'be some-body', said Hegel, one must 'belong to a particular estate'.[7]

He meant 'somebody' not in the sense of status, but of identity, and 'estate' not in the sense of a social class, but of a set of social relationships. The unsnobbish ideology of Hegel is, I hope, confirmed by a remark in *The Unfinished Revolution: How the Modernisers saved the Labour Party* by Philip Gould, one of the chief theorists of New Labour. Mr Gould describes how, as a postgraduate student in the early 1970s, 'I studied Hegel, and for the first time found a system of ideas with which I felt comfortable.' He approvingly quotes the master:

> The human being finds his proper identity only... in his membership in a group or social class whose institutions, organisation and values determine his very individuality.[8]

Labour have not followed this principle in office, but the principle is right. We each have different communities: one sort is geographical, in the heterogeneous community of our neighbourhood; another sort is more disparate and 'virtual', in the homogeneous community of 'people like us', be they aristocrats, Sikhs or skate-boarders. Most associations, of course, are blends of both sorts. And if they are healthy associations, their unconscious, subterranean effect is to strengthen the foundations of civil society in general—to disseminate (and slowly, by a complex process of testing and revision, to modify) the mores of the country as a whole. Few institutions survive today with a purpose as explicit as that of the drinking societies and correspondence clubs of the eighteenth and nineteenth centuries which, according to their articles of association, existed to do honour to King and constitution. But just as the real appeal of such associations lay in the opportunity they afforded for conviviality and community, so today the reverse applies: our modern clubs, our charities and churches, appear to exist purely for their own, private purposes, yet they unconsciously distil and disperse a more general public patriotism.

This is the value of fraternity. It is the spirit of unofficial co-operation, aimed not at general formulations or national policies but at specific actions and local needs. It should not be imagined that the shift from one to the other can be undertaken easily. A simple evacuation by the state would not cause new independent institutions to spring up automatically. The task is at once harder and less convulsive than this: to change state institutions into social ones by a sort of reverse alchemy—artificial into natural matter.

For all its difficulties, this is a bracing vision. Rather than the large, uniform outposts of central government, imagine a community populated by small, variable, local institutions, responding not to central direction but to local demand. Imagine a neighbourhood in which the schools, medical centres and welfare agencies are governed by local people; imagine if each county's police force were accountable not to the Home Office but to the people of the county itself. Imagine if social action were not the responsibility of what Alexis de Tocqueville, writing about the increasingly centralised European states of his day, called 'a powerful stranger called the government', but of individuals, families and communities themselves.[9]

'The sources of the commonwealth are in the households', Burke said simply. But what if these sources are corrupt? What if the little platoons showed no loyalty to the rest of the army? What if numbers of British citizens declined to acknowledge their obedience to the British Crown? Should they be allowed to establish or occupy the associations and institutions of a community?

The answer, easy to state but difficult to apply, is in Karl Polanyi's distinction between private and public liberty. The value of liberty is not merely—some might argue not at all—the space which it affords for private expressions, private amusements. 'Individualism,' said Polanyi, 'is no important pillar of public liberty. A free society is not an open society, but one fully dedicated to a distinctive set of beliefs.'[10] The value of liberty is the opportunity and the responsibility it gives for public virtue: the power of men and women with common ideas to band together in voluntary agreement, and build an institution to improve the quality of communal life. The Left has traditionally distrusted public liberty because it threatens the monopoly of the state in the public space, setting up alternative vehicles and sources of legitimacy for collective action. Hence the ban in communist countries on religious organisations, charities or trade unions. But it does not follow that, in a free society, any act of public liberty is to be permitted. Freedom is not an end in itself: 'even liberty', said Burke, 'must inhere in some sensible object.'[11] Social collectivism, no less than state collectivism, must chime with the national interest, with the country's common idea of the good life. Acts of public liberty must be compatible with the interests and values of British society as a whole.

Both the value and the difficulty of public liberty is its imprecision: voluntary associations are popular and effective because they are flexible to the circumstances they encounter, but for the same reason it is impossible to draw clear rules for the way in which they should work in society. However, we see here the outlines of a settlement between, on the one hand, the freedom of individuals to act in association, and on the other, the obligation on all associations which act in public to respect not only the law, but also the values and the culture, of the country as a whole.

These broad limits allow for the fullest expression of cultural diversity that any country has developed. In particular, the British demos—the collection of individuals represented in the polity—forms a civic nationalism, not an ethnic one: the British government is not, even subliminally, the leadership of a race. The point can be demonstrated by a contrast with the famous 'other': Europe. Continental states are mostly the product of nineteenth-century nationalism, of the revolt against pan-national empires. There, government was consciously conceived as the political incarnation of the French or German or Italian 'people'. In Britain, however, the state is older, and not ethnic. We date our government to the moment of foreign conquest 1,000 years ago, and our modern state to the importation of a foreign king over 300 years ago. The country is four nations under one Crown. As King John was told in Magna Carta, the pre-requisite of successful rule is that the state leaves society alone: barons have power as well as kings.

One reason for the longevity of the British political system is its secular and non-ethnic foundation. This has not dispelled either religion or patriotism; rather, it has allowed their growth, yet in a manner which has proved, mostly, positive and peaceful. The American polity, in many ways a refinement to its essentials of the British one, demonstrates this paradox best. *E pluribus unum.*

The key to our success has been that the state protects, but does not impinge upon, society—the law frames, but does not direct, the culture. Orwell was writing during the centralisation and illiberalism necessitated by total war, and yet the people he celebrated were, determinedly if unconsciously, entirely anti-statist:

> All the culture that is most truly native centres round things which even when they are communal, are not official—the pub, the football match, the back garden, the fireside and the 'nice cup of tea'.[12]

In this essay I attempt to outline the political philosophy which justifies the 'communal [but] not official'. It is necessarily abstract, a 'resort to theories', in Burke's disparaging aside. It is devoid of detailed policy, yet I hope it demonstrates that, all our common rhetoric notwith-standing, there are real differences between Right and Left, founded on very different ideas of how society works.

1

Triangulation

I blurted out the strategy I proposed in a single word: triangulate. *I found myself shaping my fingers into a triangle, with my thumbs joined at the base and my forefingers raised to meet a point at the top.*

'Triangulate, create a third position, not just in between the old positions of the two parties but above them as well…'

To demonstrate this point, I stood in front of [President Clinton] with my feet apart to represent the traditional views of the two parties. Then I stepped forward with my left foot to illustrate the new position he was shaping…

Dick Morris, Behind the Oval Office, 1997

Three 'isms'

St Stephen's Chapel, in the royal palace of Westminster, was a collegiate foundation. Like college chapels everywhere it had pews facing each other, rather than facing forward to the altar as in a parish church. So when St Stephen's became the home of the House of Commons, it was natural that friends chose to sit together, and to face their enemies across the aisle.

A two-party system is the natural product of Western politics. All attempts to overcome it—by the practical expedient of a horseshoe-shaped parliament or by the more radical method of proportional representation—seem doomed to failure. You can change the seating arrangements and you can fracture the party groupings, but Left and Right endure.

To understand Left and Right it is helpful to recognise that there are not two, but three, philosophical traditions—

three 'isms'—in modern Western politics. These are liberalism, socialism and conservatism.

Each of these traditions is, indeed, just that—a tradition, not an absolute thing. None is ever implemented in its pure and abstract form; each has its particular and diverse expressions, as well as parties and movements which take their names. And yet each *can* be summarised abstractly, for the sake of distinguishing them; each has an abstract form. In brief, then:

Liberalism is the philosophy of the *individual*. Its ethic is *liberty* and its characteristic is *autonomy*—the freedom of the will from external constraint. It says 'I shall...'.

Socialism is the philosophy of the *state*. Its ethic is *equality* and its characteristic is *coercion*—the power, in the last resort, to exert force over individuals and groups. It says 'you must...'.

Conservatism is the philosophy of *society*. Its ethic is *fraternity* and its characteristic is *authority*—the non-coercive social persuasion which operates in a family or a community. It says 'we should...'.

Of the three, conservatism is the odd man out. The individual and the state share the qualities of the ideal: pure, unchanging, noumenal, more perfect in theory than in practice. But society is real, not ideal; phenomenal, not noumenal; it is diversity, complexity and unrest.

This distinction points us to Hegel, the original triangulator. In the familiar simplification of Hegel's dialectic, a *thesis* is established which is then challenged by the *antithesis* to produce the *synthesis*, which becomes the thesis of the next stage and so on through time. Crucially, thesis and antithesis have different qualities. The thesis is Platonic, the antithesis Aristotelian: one is concept, the other experience; one is static, the other active; one is singular, the other plural; one is cold and clean, the other warm and messy. And by the mysterious process of *Aufhebung*, 'sublation', the two are reconciled. But they are not reconciled as a straight compromise or amalgam; rather, the reconciliation is the 'realisation' of the original thesis. Left alone in the fastness of idealised abstraction, the thesis is not something but merely a blueprint of something. Only when it is challenged and reformed by the phenomenal antithesis, does the noumenal thesis 'find itself', in Hegel's words: 'the new and true object arises'; it becomes 'what it intrinsically is'. The synthesis is the realised thesis, 'continually richer in itself'.[1]

How does this airy philosophy relate to practical politics? The answer is that Western politics is a dialectic process, a struggle between a pair of rival theses for sublation in the common antithesis. The thesis of the Right is the individual. The thesis of the Left is the state. And the antithesis is the same for both. It is the population *en masse*, diverse, fluid and restless: it is society. Like a pair of sperms battering at a single egg, Left and Right are each determined to plant their nature in the fertile other, in society; to perpetuate themselves, and be translated once more from the latent to the real.

The two approaches might be briefly summarised as follows. The Right-dialectic has the individual (thesis) eternally interacting with society (antithesis) in a process, *Aufhebung*, which successively delivers a modified—a socialised, a 'realised'—individuality at each stage. The pure abstraction of the solitary man, lacking association or identity, gives way to a man fulfilled in social membership. The Left-dialectic, on the other hand, has the state (thesis) being constantly modified by social realities (antithesis) but essentially, with every step, reinforcing its own centrality.

The two approaches appear close together in the competition for office only because the dialectic process—

not to mention the electoral process which reflects it—requires them to accommodate the nuanced realities of society into their rival offerings. But these offerings are based on fundamentally divergent views of the way things are and should be, and this appears once the election is over: for each side returns repeatedly to its thesis. The Right always honours the individual, and the Left always honours the state.

The Left dialectic

The recurring thesis of the Left—the successive realisation of the state through contact with the antithesis society—is most obviously apparent in the history of the Labour Party itself. This tells a story of dialectic progress from the abstraction of 'pure' statism in the first moments to the reality of 'applied' statism today.

Conceived in strict totalitarianism—revolutionary Marxism and the ideal of the dictatorship of the proletariat—the parliamentary Labour party was actually born into the democratic socialism of Kier Hardie and the Fabians. This birth represented the first accommodation with the realities of society. The party's founders were just as statist in their outlook as the revolutionaries who had gone before—envisaging the fullest degree of government control over the economic and social life of the country—but they recognised the necessity of working with the facts of the society they found themselves in, if only to change them utterly.

The first 50 years of the party's history were years of further accommodations with social reality. *Via* the staging posts of Ramsay Macdonald, the National Government and the war-time Coalition, Labour arrived at Clement Attlee and the 'mixed economy' of the post-war era. For all that Attlee's election was thought to herald the New Jerusalem, social reality soon bit: the purist Bevan did battle for the soul of the party with the realist Gaitskell, and Gaitskell won. The Bevanites achieved a symbolic victory when they stopped Gaitskell from dropping the famous Clause IV of the party's constitution (advocating the ownership by the state of the means of production, distribution and exchange), but the subsequent history of the Labour Party has conformed to the Gaitskellite, not the Bevanite tradition.

The Wilson and Callaghan era saw a further accommodation, as 'democratic socialism' degenerated into 'social democracy'. A brief and disastrous flirtation with a purer statism under the leadership of Michael Foot in the early 1980's confirmed to the party the need for another profound rapprochement with the facts of life: the long Thatcherite hegemony revealed a society even less prepared than its predecessors to accept the degree of state idealism wished for by the purists of the Left. It took fifteen years, but the Labour Party has now been 'renewed'—to use their favourite term—by the modernisers of New Labour.

Tony Blair and Gordon Brown achieved what Gaitskell failed to do: they persuaded their party to abandon Clause IV. This moment (in 1995) represented a formal renunciation of the ideal statism of the party's founders, and a public declaration of Labour's understanding of and submission to the realities of life. The result has been triumphant electoral success, unprecedented in the party's history, and a sense widely felt among the population that New Labour is as unlike Old Labour as the Conservatives themselves: that we have, in effect, an ersatz Tory government.

In this the population is mistaken, and the error is what sustains New Labour in office. This is not a substitute Tory government, but a government of the Left—as is apparent by viewing things through the prism of the dialectic. For it is precisely by means of its slow and painful accommodation with the messy realities of the antithesis-society that the thesis-state has furthered its own purposes. It has been 'realised'. The abandonment of the text of Clause IV was prelude and prerequisite to the triumph of its spirit. By renouncing its idealised abstraction the state has worked its ends on us, and become, rather than the object of remote musings by the intellectuals, the agent of awesome power over society in general.

To Old Labour, unversed in Hegel, the history of their party is the history of one shameful surrender after another, and the names MacDonald, Gaitskell and Blair are the names of traitors to the purity of the cause. To the Platonists of the Left, history is the history of degeneration, from heady idealism to disappointing reality. Mr Blair is surely right to lament this perverse historiography, the spirit within Labour which sees success and power as evidence of compromise with the enemy.* The ideology of the Left has become less romantic with every generation—and more effective.

As Labour relinquished its ambition to run every factory in the national interest, we have seen the steady surrender of what used to be called the 'commanding heights' of the economy. But the retreat from the mountains has been an invasion of the plains, where ordinary people live. The state is now a far more pervasive presence in our lives than it was ever intended to be even by Marx, whose paradoxical dialectic actually foresaw, in the socialist utopia, the withering away of the state altogether. That is hardly envisaged now.

And yet the invasion of the plains—the nationalisation of ordinary life—required a different strategy, different weapons, to those which aimed at the control of industry. In

---

* In his 2003 Party Conference speech the Prime Minister regretted that 'there has been a ritual to Labour Governments. Euphoria on victory. Hard slog in Government. Tough times. Party accuses leadership of betrayal. Leadership accuses Party of ingratitude. Disillusion. Defeat.'

Hegelian manner, the key message in New Labour's rhetoric is the need for the state to step out of its idealised fastness and into the sphere of real life.

So the Labour Party has accepted the principle of free enterprise and makes much of civil society; the Left has remembered its roots in the trade unions and has discovered a rhetoric about crime and the family which stresses communal order over individual license, and the natural efficacy of society over the coercive instrumentalism of the state. And so the rival expressions of politics, Tory and Labour, have begun to sound rather similar; it is often hard to distinguish the different theoretical skeletons beneath the flabby communitarian language.

Yet the distinctions are there. For Labour, the sphere of society—of family and order and private enterprise—is an adjunct to the sphere of the state. They wish, in a word central to their politics, for a 'partnership' between state and society, between the government on one hand, and family or business or community organisation on the other. As shall be seen, the Right has another relationship in mind—not of the state, but of the *individual* and society. For the Left's dialectic does not work.

Central to the Hegelian concept of *Aufhebung* or 'sublation' is the 'preservation' of the antithetic stages passed through by the thesis. Not only is the thesis 'realised' by its sublation: the antithesis too is strengthened and perpetuated. But the thesis only preserves those elements of the antithesis it finds conducive to itself—there must be, in the key Hegelian word, an 'ethical' relationship between thesis and antithesis, by which one relates to the other in a natural and organic manner. There is not such a relationship between the thesis state and the antithesis society.

The history of civil society in the twentieth century—the century of socialism's descent from idealism to realism—was one of steady encroachment by the state into the private sphere of commercialism and voluntarism. As a result we have seen the demise of many small and particular charities and associations whose purposes or methods the state finds inimical to its own (such as grammar schools and private care homes). We have seen the suborning of large once-independent institutions to the imperatives of national government (such as the large charities now effectively in thrall to the state). And more recently we have seen the creation of a raft of hybrid organisations, nominally independent but in fact symbiotic (or even parasitic) appendages of the public sector (such as 'Public-Private Partnerships', Network Rail or foundation hospitals).

What went wrong? At the heart of the Left dialectic is the Platonic mistake: the belief that a single wisdom—the state—is capable of directing the multifarious agencies of society. Put another way, we are witnessing, once again, the failure of universal principles of pure theory to address and accommodate the messy realities of the particular and quotidian. What is needed, instead, is a set of rules and conventions which enable this accommodation, which prevents the crash of Platonic speculation into Aristotelian reality and makes their meeting safe and fruitful. And this set of rules is what, buried beneath the accretions of recent mistakes, Britain still has.

The Right dialectic

Thomas Hobbes, writing in the 1640s in favour of an omnipotent and totalitarian state to keep men from each other's throats, asked rhetorically 'where has there been a Kingdom long free from sedition and civil war?'[2] To which the answer is, almost no-where in the world, except England since Hobbes's own day. He cannot have known it when, in the middle of the Civil War, he wrote *Leviathan*, but England was about to emerge into three and a half centuries (and counting) of peaceful political and constitutional development. And this was not because the country submitted to the rule of the totalitarian Hobbesian state. It was because, shortly after Hobbes finished writing, liberty and authority were each properly established. In the Glorious Revolution of 1688-9 (when Parliament effectively sacked the King and hired a new one on more sensible terms) what might be called the Right-dialectic—the alliance of liberalism and conservatism—was permanently instituted in the culture of the kingdom.

For three centuries, well into the twentieth, this was the dynamic of English and British history. The state was small, and played a supervisory not an active role—in the untiring metaphor of liberal and conservative alike, it was the umpire, not a player in the game. The players were individual (represented politically by the Whigs then the Liberals) and society (represented by the Tories then the Conservatives), one struggling for liberty and the other for authority in a process which progressively realised them both. The synthesis was a natural and beneficent one.

Even in the twentieth century, after the rise of Labour, this synthesis held. Liberalism very properly declined to combine with the upstart party of socialism, and joined its old adversary and natural ally, conservatism.[†] In consequence the

---

[†] By 'liberalism' I mean the philosophy, not the party which bears its name. The Liberal Party wavered all through the first half of the twentieth century over whether they were friends of the socialists or the conservatives—the daughter of their greatest leader, David Lloyd George, became a Tory while his son joined Labour—and it was not until the 1951 election that the bulk of the formerly Liberal vote finally switched to the Tories. Since then the party named Liberal—and now 'Liberal Democrat'—has been more friendly to the socialists; though there is now a strong contingent within the Parliamentary party which is ideologically aligned with the Conservatives.

British Conservative Party has acquired a healthy tone of liberalism, especially economic liberalism. And this helps explain why the Conservatives 'won' the twentieth century in Britain and 'lost' it in Europe: because in Britain the forces of the Right were united and in Europe they were divided. Simply put, in Europe there are commonly two parties of the Right: an urban, liberal, generally secular, businessmen's party and a rural, conservative, often religious, peasants' party; the effect of the separation has been the long ascendancy on the continent of the social democratic Left. In Britain, by contrast, liberals and conservatives have long been partners. The twentieth century saw united in one party's philosophy the importance of personal freedom with the imperative of family and community stability—of individual and society. The constant renewal of this alliance is the task of the Right, for the task of the Left is to disrupt it.

The governing assumption of New Labour is that the party 'lost' the twentieth century because it was divorced from its natural partner, the Liberals. What Philip Gould calls the 'forces of progress'—socialism and liberalism— were split, allowing the Conservatives a long undeserved hegemony which it is the purpose—indeed, the secret 'project'—of 'progressive politics' to end once and for all.[3]

It is central to the dogma of New Labour that the alliance of individual and society is an unnatural, indeed contradictory one. 'Devotion to the free market on one hand, and to the traditional family and nation on the other, is self-contradictory', says Anthony Giddens in *The Third Way*, a sentiment echoed throughout the literature of New Labour.[4] The myth is well-established that liberty and authority are incompatible, that individualistic enterprise is incompatible with social authority.

To be sure, liberty and authority are in tension, but they are emphatically not incompatible: they are complementary,

21

in exactly the same way that the autonomous individual complements and is complemented by—even as he struggles against—his own family. Put another way, the 'free market' depends on the values of trust and reciprocity which are generated by 'the traditional family and nation'.

The alliance the Right is devoted to is the alliance which—while other countries experimented with various forms of totalitarianism, interspersed with revolution and anarchy—sustained the peaceful political development, unparalleled social stability and enormous commercial growth of England and Britain from the seventeenth century till the twentieth. The triangular synthesis we seek is not a further development of what New Labour is pleased to call the 'partnership' of state and society: it is the natural, historic synthesis, the ancient alliance of *individual* and society.

2

Liberty and Equality

Adam was created a perfect man, his mind and body in full possession of their strength and reason.

John Locke, Second Treatise of Government, 1690

The man in isolation

The Right dialectic begins with a thesis, abstract and unreal: the 'man in isolation'. This is the individual, whose individuality is so intensified that he is literally alone. Yet he is a fully-developed adult, as Locke described Adam.

Of course (the Creation story aside) this man never existed in the flesh. And as I shall explain in due course—and as Locke and all true liberals recognise—the attempt actually to become such a person is a sociopathic attempt to escape from all the contingent limitations which make us human. The solitary man exists—as all theses exist—simply as an idea: in Burke's scornful words, 'stripped of every relation, in all the nakedness and solitude of metaphysical abstraction'.[1]

And yet the isolated individual is of central importance, for he exists deep within each of us, in the privacy of our reflective consciousness. The workings of our own minds are, to us, essentially 'metaphysical'. Our natural state really is one of 'nakedness', unclothed by assumed virtue or sophistication or learning; 'solitude' is the primary fact of our lives, be we never so gregarious. And as rational creatures who yearn for freedom and objectivity, to be 'stripped of every relation' is indeed our mental (though not our emotional) goal. This is apparent in intellectual matters: we seek to free ourselves from 'subjectivity' and 'prejudice'

23

in order to gain the 'truth', which is (classically understood, at least) something independent of our personal position. It is even more apparent in moral matters where, as Kant observed, our attempts to behave in the 'right' way are attempts to extrude all that is particular to us, to ignore our own interests and affections in our assessment of what to do: to behave, in short, as a pure, ideal, rational individual, 'stripped of every relation', might behave.[2]

The notion of the man in isolation prompts that famous device of liberal philosophy, the 'social contract'. This is the imagined deal by which the individual has consented to be ruled by government so long as his basic autonomy is recognised and safeguarded. The contract is often placed in the mythic past, as the first social act of our ancestors. For this reason it is generally reviled by conservatives as abstract theorising: the empirical instinct and the mystical instinct, equally strong in the conservative mentality, both revolt at such a dogmatic and clear-cut treatment of pre-history. As Roger Scruton has argued, the idea implies a rationalism and unity of purpose in our collective ancestry which itself presumes an organised society.[3] But to reject the concept of a contract on these grounds is to take it too literally. As Hume said, the contract is nowhere written—'but we trace it plainly in the nature of men'.[4] Historically nebulous it may be, but the idea enables us formally to identify the natural boundary between ourselves and others. The social contract is not a chronological account but a philosophical explanation: not a judgment of 'which came first'—the individual or society—but a simple recognition that we are separate from our fellows. There was not a vast ceremony at some primeval Runnymede, when the entire community solemnly foreswore selfishness and submitted to a constitutional monarchy; but there is a private understanding in the heart of each of us that we are only sociable *conditionally*: we want our life, liberty, and property to be ours alone.

These three attributes—life, liberty and property—occupy a sacred place in the liberal philosophy because they are the only attributes which one can definitely say the man in isolation has. In that unpopulated state there is nothing to give him character or consciousness other than the promptings of his own nature (which we can hardly guess at), for he has had no nurture at all. All that is known is negative: no man can murder him, confine him, or steal from him. He is safe from attack, he can wander at will, and what he has (a horse, a house, a mountain) he holds.

Rights and responsibilities

The attributes of life, liberty and property constitute *rights*. No more confusing or misused term exists in politics, because so little recognition is given to its true provenance: rights are the attributes of the man in isolation which are retained into his social existence. In the famous phrases of the American Declaration of Independence, they are 'self-evident' and 'inalienable'. They do not require the existence of other men to make them exist: they are demonstrably there in the circumstances of a human life. And no man can alienate—surrender to others—his rights to life, liberty and property. In a state of isolation he would actually be unable to do so, and in a state of society he would not willingly do so. He might, for some reason, willingly surrender the things themselves—his property, his liberty or even his life—but he would not surrender his *right* to them: the power of decision, the right to decide on the surrender of the things themselves, he retains. To surrender the right would be an act of abnegation impossible in nature—possible at all, perhaps, only in love.

25

The concept of a right as something retained, rather than granted, makes the individual sovereign—and so makes him responsible. The solitary provenance of rights means that the 'right' carries the 'responsibility'. The man in isolation is not only safe from murder, imprisonment or theft: he is incapable of visiting these depredations on other people. The same circumstances which protect him, constrain him.

New Labour's frequent avowal of the link between 'rights and responsibilities' hints at, but misses this truth. Their rhetoric implies that the transaction is a *quid pro quo* of two contrasting qualities: that rights are given by the state *in exchange for* the exercise of responsibility by the individual. The Right's idea, by contrast, is that rights and responsibilities are not simply linked, but the same thing, seen from the position of subject or object. A right is not a privilege, to be paid for by some formal obeisance to the community: it is the natural attribute of the individual who emerged from isolation with his sovereignty and his responsibility intact and indivisible. Responsibility, as Hegel emphasised, is not merely a 'moral… *obligation*', but an ethical '*fact*'; we cannot coherently claim our rights without acknowledging our responsibilities.[5]

Real rights can be distinguished from false rights simply in this, that with real rights the same person who carries the freedom (or the entitlement), carries the responsibility (or the obligation). With false rights—such as the 'right' to be provided with income, or to behave in a certain way—the balance is otherwise: one person carries the freedom and another (usually everyone else) carries the responsibility. I have a 'right' to an income: you have a responsibility to provide me with it. I have a 'right' to behave as I wish: you have an obligation not to interfere or complain. A real right, by contrast, enforces a restraint on its possessor, requiring him simply to mind his own business, and so to respect the rights of others. The same 'fact' which entitles me to my life, liberty and property, obliges me to respect yours.

For the same reason, rights pertain to individuals, not to groups. Because the attributes they protect belonged originally to a solitary man, rights in a state of society belong to all people rather than to some: they are not privileges, but the essence of equality. You often hear the formulation: 'the rights of…' some particular body or group. But rights apply to individuals qua individuals, denuded of associative or 'group' identity. Not our particular characteristics brings us our rights, but our status as subjects of the state. This was the argument of John Stuart Mill's proto-feminist tract *On the Subjection of Women*, which he neatly illustrated by his attempt, as a Member of Parliament, to enfranchise women with a simple amendment to the wording of the 1867 Reform Act, changing 'man' to 'person'.[6] 'Right', said Hegel, 'is that which remains indifferent to particularity.'[7]

Equality and the law

The dialectical narrative has the individual emerging from isolation with his basic sovereignty—the sanctity of his rights to life, liberty and property—intact. Now, if the translation from solitude to society were simply a translation to another state of abstraction, then the others the individual joins, being similarly idealised, similarly 'stripped of every relation', would be equal to him in every respect: they would be identical. Society would be, as Locke put it, a state of 'equality, wherein all the power… is reciprocal, no-one having more than another.' Each identical man would recognise, without prompting or demonstration, the rights of all the others to their life, liberty and property; we would have a state of nature governed by 'good-will, [and] mutual assistance', in which autonomy was regulated by 'calm reason and conscience', and every one worked together for the general good.[8]

As Locke recognised, however, reality operates differently. The emergence from solitude to society is a fraught business, as the purity of the thesis is challenged by the messy realities of the antithesis. The abstract individual, brought into the solid reality of a social existence, does not naturally observe those limits on his autonomy which, in the metaphorical state of isolation, circumstances imposed on him; nor do 'calm reason and conscience' operate with quite the degree of efficacy Locke wished for. The idealised abstract individual which in our inmost minds we strive to represent figures forth in each of us with a whole character of difference. The other individuals we come across are neither identical to us in strength and understanding, nor necessarily disposed to recognise our sacred rights to life, liberty, and property. The result—the 'state of nature' which would exist in the absence of organised, political or 'civil' society—is surely not 'good will'. It would be, as Hobbes foresaw, a life of nastiness, poverty, brutality and brevity, a 'war of every man against every man', where the strong domineer over the weak and the weakest go to the wall.[9]

Enter Leviathan. The process of emerging from the state of nature is the process of submitting to another form of restraint but one's own dim conscience and the violence of others. For Hobbes, this was simply 'a common power, to keep men in awe': Leviathan is the omnipotent agency of an arbitrary government, deriving its legitimacy from the idea of statutory power, anointed and absolute, set out in the Old Testament.[10] Locke, on the other hand, envisaged not so much a 'common power' as 'a standing rule to the live by'. His contribution to our politics was to limit the power of the state by deriving its legitimacy from below. The 'standing rule' is not principally a coercive force, a Leviathan, but a common agreement, imposing a moral duty of conformity as well as a threat of violence in the case of disobedience. Furthermore, Locke insisted that as well as the public, the state itself is also governed by the law. 'Laws not men should rule'.[11]

If the principal attribute of the individual is liberty—the autonomy retained from the state of isolation—that of the state is equality. The relation of the two is straightforward. The purpose of the state, acting on behalf of the law, is to uphold the social contract, to enforce on each individual the basic equality with which he emerged into society. Justice is blind: it has regard purely for the individual before it, whom it takes to be free and self-responsible and possessed of the inalienable rights to life, liberty and property. It ignores all other factors, all group identities and private characteristics which flesh out the legal abstraction 'man'. In Kantian terms, it suborns us all to the categorical imperative.

Property

By limiting our freedom equally, the law renders our freedom conducive to the good of others; we become not threats to, but agents of, their well-being. Most of all it makes the accumulation and distribution of property a collaborative exercise. Far from being an isolating phenomenon, separating man from man in a world of atomistic selfishness, the use of liberty in the disposal of property— the free market, in short—is the most co-operative endeavour mankind engages in. Adam Smith's *Wealth of Nations* devotes two pages, replete with joyful exclamation marks, to the provenance of 'the woollen coat, which covers the day-labourer', listing all the people and trades which go into making it, and all the people and trades which make the tools required for making it and the means required for transporting it, citing the 'assistance and co-operation of many thousands' who, in unthinking concert, deliver such a vital item, at an affordable price, to the poorest sort of man.[12]

The contribution of the rule of law to the wealth of nations is apparent in the famous work of the Peruvian economist Hernando de Soto, who shows how the poverty of under-developed countries flows from the absence of property rights there: without state recognition of the ownership of assets, all the freedom to buy and sell counts for little.[13]

But the need for state *recognition* of property does not justify state *appropriation* of it. The Right recognises the importance of property ownership to be such that compulsory redistribution, beyond a very limited degree, is an offence against society itself. Ownership, as Roger Scruton says, relates individuals to circumstances, to the natural world and to others: without it we have no solid relationships with life. Under a propertied dispensation, as he puts it, man 'is now at home where before he was merely let loose.' Property constitutes the 'socialising of objects', the putting them to purposes, as it were, beyond themselves, as articles of trade, security and status: through ownership 'the object is lifted out of mere thinghood and rendered up to humanity'.[14]

To humanity, note—not just to the owner. As Aristotle explained, when the ownership of property is private, 'the use of it [is] communal'. The rich have a social, not a statutory obligation to help the poor; a statutory obligation, fulfilled through large-scale compulsory redistribution, damages the very basis of the social principle. The abolition of the right of property, Aristotle warned, would do away with two fundamental social virtues: self-restraint on the part of the owner, and liberality or generosity toward others.[15] It would also, as de Soto has demonstrated, impoverish the world.

Social justice as 'equality'

Of course, capitalism has its detractors. Far from being co-operative, it is argued, the free market is exploitative; far from being egalitarian, it produces unequal accumulations of wealth, from the degradingly poor to the disgustingly rich. And though the world still waits for an alternative that will work, in one important respect the detractors of capitalism have a point. The scheme outlined hitherto is a limited one. Equality under the law, the categorical imperative, the defence of our rights, the power to use liberty in the disposal of property—all this is not enough.

The law might return us to our original isolation by uniformly upholding our rights, but beyond this it does not affect our relations or our lives. It enables free movement and the free transmission of property, but it does no more than that. The law, baldly operating, has no response—is blind—to the accidental circumstances which messy, antithetic society throws up and which, as individuals, we are often incapable of affecting. The law can stop us killing, imprisoning or stealing from each other; beyond these negative protections, it cannot make us healthy, wealthy or happy, or prevent the opposite of these boons befalling us. It cannot prevent outrages against moral feeling which fall outside the sphere of individual justice. And this is why we want more than equality under the law, more than individual justice. We want *social* justice too.

Right and Left disagree fundamentally over the meaning and method of social justice. Many on the Right disagree with the very term—which enables many on the Left to claim it as their own. 'To be on the Left', says Anthony Giddens, 'is to be concerned… with the pursuit of social justice'.[16] Perhaps so; yet the reverse is not true: one can also be concerned with the pursuit of social justice and not 'on the Left'. The Right have a claim here too.

For the Left, Professor Giddens defines social justice in two ways, one of them axiomatic to the old Left, the other to the new Left. The old Left, and more familiar meaning of the term is 'equality'. By this is meant not only equality in our basic *rights* but also in our actual *circumstances*. Social justice, in this view, means the extension of the egalitarian principle of the law out of the sphere of individual rights and into the sphere of social relations. The quality pertaining to our abstract individuality—our equal identical sameness—is applied to our concrete lives: we are to be made equal not only in our rights to things, but in the things themselves.

And what is the procedure for this operation? The same as the other. The agency which enforces the abstract individual law—the state—assumes further ambitions. Where the blind, impartial law sought to return us to egalitarian *abstraction* in order to deliver *individual* justice, the percipient, partial state seeks to force us into egalitarian *reality*, in order to deliver *social* justice.

The method by which the Left extend the principle of individual rights into the sphere of social relations is shown most clearly in the famous 'theory of justice' of the Harvard philosopher John Rawls. Rawls begins where all proper liberals begin: with the Kantian principle of the idealised, abstract individual, standing behind a 'veil of ignorance' which obscures to him and us everything that gives him identity and particularity—with the man in isolation, in short. Rawls' conceit is this: that were the man asked to define the political and legal characteristics of the world he is to live in, he would (because he is entirely ignorant of his own strengths or status in it) choose characteristics most conducive to the good of all. 'Each is forced to choose for everyone.'[17]

That might be the rationale of the man in isolation—but what sort of society, in practice, would he choose?

According to Rawls, he would choose socialism, or something near to it.

The first of Rawls' famous 'two principles of justice' is the essential liberal one: that 'each person has an equal right to the most extensive basic liberty compatible with a similar liberty for others'; one cannot interpret this 'basic liberty' as other than the right to life, liberty and property. It is on his second principle that both the conservative and the true liberal depart from Rawls: his ignorant man, he suggests, would also demand that 'social and economic inequalities are to be arranged so that they are to the greatest benefit of the least advantaged'. And to Rawls this means an egalitarian economic agenda. He is not so illiberal or fantastical to demand the absence of all inequality (he concedes the truth that sometimes the lot of all can be improved by some people proceeding faster than others, as risk-taking pathfinders and innovators) but he wishes to ensure that the only inequalities which are tolerated are those which conduce to the good of the worst-off. And it is the state which must decide what these are.

Rawls' first principle is liberal; his second is socialist. The difference is this: while the first is objective, focusing on the 'equal right' of 'each person', the second is subjective, focusing on 'social and economic' *circumstances*. What begins in solitary abstraction ends in the sphere of human relations—and the agent of the second principle, as of the first, is the state.

'The imaginary rights of men', observed Burke, are 'a confusion of judicial with civil principles'.[18] It is the deceptive trick of the Left to apply the appearance of procedural and impartial 'justice' to discriminatory and arbitrary power. Rawls claims that his theory—which he calls 'justice as fairness'—proceeds directly from the Kantian ideal, from the 'original position' in which the individual lacks all personality and particularity. As Rawls puts it, his theory enables us to 'use the idea of pure procedural justice from the beginning', and so to 'strive for a kind of moral geometry'.[19] The metaphor should alarm. Hobbes, too, sought 'principles of Reason' in politics which reflected the rules of 'arithmetic and geometry'; he, too, founded his philosophy on the liberal principle of individual autonomy and he, too, worked from there to a justification of full-blown tyranny.[20] Where Hobbes feared 'war', Rawls fears 'unfairness'; but the analysis is the same, and the result. Rawls' theory is a recipe for the most swingeing redistribution of property and the most thorough curtailment of liberty.

It is the 'confusion of judicial with civil principles' which accounts for Left-wing social policy: the concentration of power in the hands of the state, which is necessary in judicial matters, is also applied in social ones. The state's rightful monopoly on the use of force—the ultimate judicial sanction—becomes a monopoly on almost everything else.

Social justice as 'emancipation'

If Professor Giddens' first meaning for social justice is the 'Old Labour' principle of 'equality', extended from the sphere of individual rights to the sphere of social circumstances, his second is more recognisably 'New Labour'. This is the 'emancipation' of the individual. People, he says, should have 'autonomy of action'—they must be free to define their own lives, independent of social custom or economic circumstance.

In this twin definition we see the New Labour 'project': the attempt to link the two 'progressive' traditions of socialism and liberalism, of equality and individualism. The two are, Professor Giddens argues, closely related:

egalitarian measures often increase the range of freedoms open to individuals. Freedom to social democrats should mean autonomy of action, which in turn demands the involvement of the wider social community.[21]

So, not only (*vide* Rawls) is the liberal ethic of individual rights twisted into a justification for the extension of the egalitarian state into the sphere of social relations, but egalitarian measures are justified on the grounds of the assistance they can give to the liberation—the emancipation—of the individual.

As noted, liberalism and egalitarianism, the free individual and the coercive state, are properly and naturally allied in the social contract. In a truly liberal society, statutory coercion is exercised for the sake of individual freedom, in the form of pure, procedural, individualistic law. The state simply guarantees the individual's right to life, liberty and property.

But we see now that there can also be a less fruitful alliance between the individual and the state. When the state steps out of its proper bounds, and attempts to deliver not only objective individual justice, but subjective, social justice too, the change brings the individual out of his life of law-regulated rectitude and spurs him to embark on a quite different career. He becomes the object not of protection, but of solicitation by the state; he is encouraged to believe—is even legally required to act on the belief—that he has certain 'rights' vis-à-vis his fellows which it is his duty (his only one) to exact the performance of. He is encouraged to look to the state not purely for the guarantee of his basic rights but for the satisfaction of all his wants. Of course, this necessitates the sacrifice of much liberty. But the liberty is in areas (education, healthcare, income) where the accompanying responsibility weighs heavily, and the reward of the sacrifice is an immediate 'entitlement' to those things formerly only gained by the sweat of his brow; it is an easy sacrifice, and one justified, moreover, under the pious heading of 'equality'. Finally, the deal is concluded with an extension of liberty into areas which, under the old dispensation of self-responsibility, suffered the strictest curtailment by law and public opinion: the boundless areas of 'self-expression'.

Of course, belief in self-determination and personal autonomy—in 'being your own person', 'taking orders from no-one', 'not caring what people think'—is a particularly English characteristic, remarked on by foreigners throughout our modern history as the glory of a country which had freedom under the law. But it was, until recently, a characteristic with a corollary. The staples of the national caricature, the rumbustious English sailor, the eccentric English gentlemen, the iconoclastic English aesthete, all understood what they were rebelling against. Self-determination was qualified by self-restraint; the autonomy exercised in the name of private liberty deferred to the prevailing culture. No longer. Self-expression has become something much nastier and more assertive. Many consider liberty to be in implacable enmity with the very notion of a prevailing culture; to defer to anything is entirely out of the question. Contempt for bourgeois morality is becoming the prevailing atmosphere of bourgeois society.

This was not the way the Left began: 'equality' did not always admit of 'emancipation'. Marx may have been a wild young man in his youth, but with age he acquired gravitas, and imparted it to the movement he inspired. The founding tradition of the Labour Party was the Puritanism of the Webbs. Sidney and Beatrice—their dreary attitude famously summed up in Beatrice's diary entry, 'a useful little dinner party'—frowned on liberalism. They preferred the regimented austerity of the state to the frivolity and selfishness of individual freedom. But in the post-war years this mood gave way to something more fun. As Anthony Crosland put it in *The Future of Socialism*, there must be space, alongside Fabian respectability, for 'grace and gaiety':

> Posthumously, the Webbs have won their battle, and converted a generation to their standard. Now the time has come for a reaction: for a greater emphasis on private life, on freedom and dissent, on culture, beauty, leisure, and even frivolity. Total abstinence and a good filing-system are not now the sign-posts to the socialist's Utopia: or at least, if they are, some of us will fall by the way-side.[22]

Crosland's message was heeded by the government of Harold Wilson, and especially by the Home Secretary, Roy Jenkins, who legalised homosexuality, liberalised the divorce laws and relaxed the rules on censorship. These reforms were salutary, marking a decisive break with the top-down, conformist conservatism of the previous era. Jenkins enacted a toleration of noncomformity in private life, a central element in true liberalism. Today, however, the *soi-disant* liberals who look to Crosland and Jenkins for their inspiration go a step farther, and so leave true liberalism behind.

In short, they have not confined themselves to repealing statutory injunctions against 'dissent'—they have introduced statutory injunctions against *social* injunctions against dissent. As Burke put it, 'they take the deviation from the rule for the rule itself'. They propose not the *toleration* of dissent but its *normalisation*: political correctness formalised, made compulsory. This is not liberalism, for when deviation becomes the rule there can be no deviation from *that*; no grace, gaiety or frivolity then.

So 'emancipation', in the Left's view, means the emancipation of the individual from the trammels of society. And this betrays a misunderstanding of the nature of freedom itself. For if one article of freedom (as the manumission decree for slaves in ancient Greece put it) is the 'right to movement according to [one's] own choice', this does not mean that the most frantic and aimless peripatetic is the freest man imaginable. On the contrary, an aimless peripatetic could hardly be said to be free at all.

It has been remarked that when men cease to believe in God, they do not then believe in nothing: they believe in anything. The same goes for social beliefs and allegiances. Denied a cultural context, denied the authority which makes his freedom meaningful, a man is not free but merely whimsical. He becomes, as Hegel warned, the 'plaything of raging elements', a slave to 'the subjective vanity of feeling and the arbitrariness of caprice.'[23] A man freed from all restraint is not 'autonomous'—self-determining—but 'heteronomous', subject to whatever external or internal stimuli chance along. He is not free, but in hopeless thrall to impulse and circumstances, driven by the most basic urgings of his nature into a parody of liberation: shopping and copulating—getting and begetting—his way through life and prey to any passing will stronger than his own. And so he has all the independence of the man in isolation but none of the natural safeguards which made the solitary man harmless: lack of opportunity, lack of others. This man is dangerous.

Of course, few individuals are so completely indifferent to their culture, so out of sympathy with their social context, that they operate in this terrible way. There has, however, been a dangerous attenuation of the intellectual, and consequently the practical, link between personal behaviour and social justice; between one's private decisions and the state of the public space. We have pushed the moral sphere away from the individual, and loaded the onus for good behaviour onto remote agents in the large organisations, the governments and corporations. The conscience is satisfied by some abstract commitment to a global campaign, signified perhaps by the wearing of a charity wristband; the will is freed of what it rejoices to regard as the illegitimate, socially controlling, patriarchal dominance of culture.

The point is made, approvingly, by Anthony Giddens:

> Surveys show that younger generations today are sensitised to a greater range of moral concerns than previous generations were. They do not, however, relate these values to tradition, or accept traditional forms of authority as legislating on questions of lifestyle. Some such moral values are clearly post-materialist… concerning for example ecological values, human rights or sexual freedom.[24]

The confusion here is of morality with moralism. Left-liberalism makes us more *moralistic* than our parents and grandparents—in the sense of relating more questions of human conduct to moral criteria—but it makes us decidedly less *moral*—in the sense of doing the right thing by our families and our neighbours. The questions we relate to moral criteria are questions which, by and large, do not concern ourselves, are not 'questions of lifestyle': indeed the whole of our modern moral position might be summed up in the dictum that moral rules are for others to obey.

The ethic of Left-liberalism imposes its weight on others, while enlarging our own sphere of freedom. 'Ecological values' and 'human rights' require other people—businesses, governments—to behave well to the planet and the poor; 'sexual freedom' simply requires other people—neighbours, governments—not to interfere with me. As a moral code it is a remarkably easy one to abide by, especially for a young person with no responsibilities. Indeed, as Giddens says, it is the morality of 'post-materialism': when material considerations are taken care of, by a beneficent government or one's beneficent parents, this is the sort of morality that is championed.

Today's middle-aged, the former rebels of the 1960s and 1970s, rebelled against a society which was secure. It is often pointed out that hippies came disproportionately from stable, middle-class homes. Disaffection with the prevailing order did not profoundly challenge that order, as can be seen by the easy assimilation most hippies have undergone in their maturity. Bourgeois morality could survive the rebellion and even welcome the ex-rebels, when they came to their senses, back into the fold. But that generation's children, today's young, have nothing to rebel against but the intellectual residue of nonconformity, which is all that remains of the parents' rebellion. Many, it is true, are rebelling altogether, defecting back to conservative doctrine: finding no personal resonance in the hollow vessel of liberal relativism, they have discovered for themselves the merits of social authority. But most are not so daring. The pall of social disgrace still hangs over conservatism. For many children of the *soixante-huitards* the only option is a further moral unravelling, a deeper and more despairing rebellion than that perpetrated by the parents. Filial enough to concur in the original revolt, they are sensible enough to see the emptiness of its effects. Where the parents were rebels from principle, these are rebels from *ennui*; post-modern rebels against nothing. That was a revolt for Utopia: this is a revolt for cynicism. Nothing has been created in the place of social authority; a re-creation of what is lost is out of the question; what is there for them but a celebration of irony and boredom?

Education

The two attitudes which make up the Left's definition of social justice—equality and emancipation, coercion and autonomy, *might* the noun and *might* the verb—dovetail neatly. The same culture which argues for a large state, to limit the ravages of capitalism and provide for the welfare needs of the people, also defends the absolute right of the individual to do what he likes, without repercussion, in all the decisions of his life.

Our culture is in the grip of this pernicious alliance, between the self-seeking individualism celebrated by John Stuart Mill and the bloated, all-aggrandising, all-powerful state advocated by Thomas Hobbes. Between the political avatars of *On Liberty* and *Leviathan* we are suffering the dreadful effects of an ideological pincer-movement, joined at the hinge and operated by the hand of Left-liberalism. Between the two, society is being squeezed to death.

Equality and emancipation—state socialism and individualist liberalism—each occupies the place of the thesis in the political dialectic. As such they share certain qualities, not least their common rationalism. The libertarian Robert Nozick, no less than his Harvard colleague and adversary John Rawls, applied a desiccated rationalism to the defence of the individual—emphasising above all else 'the fact of our separate existence'—which appears, in its reasoning and its results, very little different from the Rawlsian analysis he is trying to overturn.[25] Both Rawls and Nozick began with Kant's undifferentiated individual: that they arrived at opposite conclusions should not blind us to their close relation.

The common rationalism of the two theories prompts their common materialism. The economic creeds of ultra-liberalism and socialism are both founded on what Friedrich von Hayek called 'that celebrated figment… *homo economicus*'.[26] The individualist and the statist both see man as driven primarily, even purely, by the pursuit of personal profit. This caricature, often falsely attributed to Adam Smith, was in fact first sketched by Hobbes, and then in the nineteenth century filled out in their different ways by Mill and Marx.* While liberalism holds the selfish pursuit of profit to be an inevitable and therefore good thing (left to itself, the invisible hand will ensure that everyone is provided for) and socialism regards it as wholly bad (it is naked greed and conflict and the-devil-take-the-hindmost) the difference in analysis is minimal. The more nearly the two theories approach completeness the more they resemble each other: ultimately a philosophy founded on the unfettered liberation of the individual is little different from one founded on his total confinement. When the rights of individuals are utterly suborned to the 'good of all', the situation hardly differs from a state of 'every man for himself'.

'Despotism', said de Tocqueville:

---

* Hobbes, who was both the first bourgeois economist and the first state collectivist, saw the life of man as one of ceaseless material acquisitiveness: 'felicity', he thought, 'is a continual progress of the desire, from one object to another; the attaining of the former, being still but the way to the latter' (*Leviathan*, 1651). Marx's materialism was built, consciously and explicitly, on that of Adam Smith and the classical economists; the only modification he made to Smith's principles was to strip them of any non-materialist considerations. (Marx's intensification of Smith's materialism is explored in Isaiah Berlin's *Karl Marx: his life and environment*, 1939.) The limits to Smith's own materialism are apparent in the famous first lines of the *Theory of Moral Sentiments*, 1759: 'How selfish soever man may be supposed, there are evidently some principles in his nature, which interest him in the fortune of others, and render their happiness necessary to him, though he derives nothing from it except the pleasure of seeing it.' Smith did not believe man to be purely motivated by the desire for acquisition; Marx did. And Mill agreed with him. As Hayek says, the notion of *homo economicus* was 'explicitly introduced [to liberal theory], with much else that belongs to the rationalist rather than the evolutionary tradition, only by the younger Mill.' (*The Constitution of Liberty*, 1960)

sees the isolation of men as the best guarantee of its own permanence. So it usually does all it can to isolate them. Of all the vices of the human heart egoism is that which suits it best.[27]

The large state requires above all else the separation of citizens from each other; it requires that men look not to their neighbours but to the government as the only source of help, the only object of affection and the only giver of rules. And so, as Hegel said, the nation becomes '[a] soulless community... split up into a mere multiplicity of individuals... in which all count the same'.[28]

It is the purpose of the Left dialectic to subsume social responsibilities into the remit of the state. And this includes the most critical responsibility of all, that of the care and education of children. Anthony Giddens sees 'no permanent boundary between government and civil society'. More starkly, he sees a 'surprisingly close' similarity between the public sector and the family, which (a conservative would say) is the social, rather than statutory, institution *par excellence*. Ideally, says Giddens, both the public sector and the family are 'democracies', in which equality, rights and 'negotiated' (rather than 'traditional') authority operate, including in the relationship of children and parents.[29]

The logical end of this attitude is Plato's policy, by which the state suppresses the home altogether and takes over the functions of family life itself. Recent legislation authorises the establishment of universal state childcare centres. Such a system is already presaged by the system for older children: universal state schools.

Education neatly illustrates the difference between Left and Right, for each side's attitude to the subject reflects an alternative understanding of human nature. To the Platonic Left, the child is born perfect, and degenerates thereafter. To the Aristotelian Right, the child is born imperfect, and improves. In the Left's view of things, the child emerges into a world whose social and economic arrangements are such that he is (in the term Marx took from Hegel) 'alienated' from his real nature and from his fellows, and forced into an exploiting and exploited relationship with mankind. The task of education, therefore, is to counteract the processes of time and circumstance, to eliminate as determining factors all previous influences on the child's life, be they genetic, cultural or material; to undo the dialectic and return the individual to that state of abstract, identical equality which preceded his social existence.

So it was that since the 1960s a blanket of identical government schooling has been laid over the country, in which any differences between children, of ability or inclination, was deliberately, explicitly discounted. The 'slate', in Plato's phrase, was to be 'wiped clean'.[30] Comprehensive education, by redressing the corrupt circumstances of 'home' from which the child arrives at school, was designed to overcome the child's alienation and recover his prelapsarian state of innocence, equality and human kinship.

The Right, by contrast, sees the purpose of education to be melioration, not revolution. Education is the process by which the child, composed of all the natural affections and emotions, attains the secondary faculties—objectivity, self-knowledge, reason and morality itself—which civilise his basic, amoral urges. It is not the process of 'cultural control', of indoctrination in the evil ways of the grown-up; nor can education mean the liberation of the child from the corruption of society. It is the process by which the unformed individual is accommodated into the particularity and concreteness of his social context.

So the Left's idea of education is to abstract the child from the history and family which made him, and to refashion him in some alternative image of their own devising; the

Right regards education as a means of strengthening his identity, of deepening his links with his family and society and thus with himself. And so the locus of responsibility in each world-view differs. For the Left, responsibility for the child's education rests with the state, and any attempt by the child's parents to take responsibility themselves is regarded as the exploitation of unfair social and economic circumstances. To the Right, by contrast, the education of children is the supreme, almost exclusive responsibility of the parents who brought them into the world. Not the state, not 'society' in the abstract—which is the state—but the family, is rightfully responsible for a child's schooling. Parents should be in charge.

3

Fraternity

The state ought to confine itself to what regards the state... in a word, to everything that is truly and properly public, to the public peace, to the public safety, to the public order, to the public prosperity...

[Politicians] cannot do the lower duty; and, in proportion as they try it, they will certainly fail in the higher. They ought to know... what belongs to laws, and what manners alone can regulate. To these, great politicians may give a leaning, but they cannot give a law.

Edmund Burke, *Thoughts and Details on Scarcity, 1795*

Positive liberty

The English translation of Norberto Bobbio's book *Left and Right*, on which Anthony Giddens draws heavily in *The Third Way*, carries an introduction by the political scientist Allan Cameron. This perfectly expresses the way the Left conflates state with society. Stating that the two principles 'liberty and equality' have 'guided Europe since the Enlightenment', Mr Cameron adds a footnote:

> Fraternity, the other item in the French revolutionary slogan, was perhaps just rhetoric or a more emotive way of saying equality. Brothers are equal...[1]

The French revolutionaries, under whom the genuine if misapplied 'fraternity' of 1789 degenerated into the terrible 'equality' of 1792, may have agreed with Mr Cameron. But fraternity deserves more than a footnote, and better treatment than this.

The equality of brothers, Hegel reminds us, is 'an empty and tautological proposition'. We are equal precisely insofar as we are alone and disconnected from others: for 'equality… can only be the equality of abstract persons'.[2] From outside the family, to be sure—from the point of view of a detached observer, such as the state or a political scientist—brothers are indeed equal; from such a viewpoint they are also indistinguishable, the faceless entries on a census form or a tax return. To the brothers themselves, however, what matters is not their notional *equality* but their *fraternity*: their kinship, and the exclusiveness which their shared home and common memories entail. Brothers are not equal, except in that sphere of abstraction which is quite irrelevant to their daily lives: they are different, possessed of different qualities and strengths and attitudes, yet they are intimately connected to each other. In short, they are *related*.

'Relationship' is the heart of the conservative disposition. Its combination of individuality with connection—autonomy in a social context—neatly expresses the Right dialectic. More familiarly, the Right dialectic comprehends the famous 'two concepts of liberty' identified by Isaiah Berlin: one English, limited and 'negative', the other Continental, grandiose and 'positive'.[3] Negative liberty means the protection of those basic, irrefrangible qualities, the right to life, liberty and property, possessed by the man in isolation. It is negative in the sense that it lays down injunctions *against* behaviour, injunctions which apply equally to all: 'you may *not*' do such and such (kill another, confine him or steal from him, in short).

Negative freedom is blind—all people are regarded as identical and unrelated, with no distinguishing qualities or affiliations to affect the impartial handing down of justice. 'Positive' freedom, on the other hand, dwells precisely in the realm of difference and affiliation. Negative freedom, for all that it is designed to assist the social process, concerns the private individual: it erects a barrier, enclosing a space in which he is free from others. Positive freedom, however, is relational: it directly concerns the social being. Simply put, where negative freedom seeks the *liberation* of the person (by removing the threat of coercion by others) positive freedom seeks his *fulfilment* (by folding him in the embrace of others). It seeks, in Hegel's words, the 'realisation' of the individual, the emergence of his 'true' or 'best' self.[4]

It is a basic article of the liberal tradition that the legal system should be founded on the negative concept of liberty. Positive freedom, when undertaken by the state, is not relational but repressive. A state or legal establishment which has the 'fulfilment' or 'realisation' of the individual as its primary purpose—rather than simply his liberation from the threats to his life, liberty or property—has arrogated all his autonomy and all his character. This is the error of both the socialist, who wishes to 'realise' the individual by statutory action in order to 'liberate' him from economic or social bondage, and also of the authoritarian conservative or religious zealot, who wishes to use the state to enforce social or spiritual conformity. The Government takes it upon itself to perform the 'self-realisation' of the individual on his behalf; any resistance is explained as his not knowing his best interests and his true nature; it proves he is sinful, or suffering (in the Marxist phrase) 'false consciousness', or in some other way alienated from the true and the good: he must be squeezed into shape for his own sake. As Berlin said, state-led positive liberty involves a 'monstrous imper-sonation', and a monstrous tyranny.[5]

All that said, it is not enough simply to proclaim our preference for negative freedom and leave it at that. If the error of the socialist or authoritarian is to conflate society with the state, and therefore to seek the 'realisation' of the individual through his identification with the government, the error of the ultra-liberal is to decline to seek his realisation at all. The socialist and authoritarian favour the wrong alliance—individual with state—while the ultra-liberal favours no alliance at all.

Liberals are right to focus the operation of the state on the guarantee of limited individual rights; but the individual wants more than his rights. The skeleton of individualism must be clothed in the flesh and blood of identity, personality and prejudice. The isolated individual must be subjected to the dialectic: he must undergo the transformative process, be 'realised' by contact not with the coercive state, but with authoritative society. For it is society which gives a person himself, and his happiness.

The person abstracted from all contingent circumstances—the man in isolation—is not truly a man at all, merely (Hegel again) 'the sheer *empty unit* of the person'.[6] The original, Kantian individual who signs the social contract from behind the veil of ignorance, with his objective intellect and his dispassionate morality, is admirable and necessary. But he is not enough. We all wish to achieve intellectual independence of mind, and to make moral judgements which are not influenced by our personal bias—but we wish to do so as rarely as possible. Most of the time we want to *feel*, not to *think* or *judge*; most of the time, thankfully, our interests and affections, not our intellect and ethics, govern our behaviour. Intellectual and moral objectivity, truth and right, involve extruding all that is particular and specific to oneself; this is the route to rectitude, but not to happiness. Kant's ideal man, who acts in all things according to the categorical imperative, referring his decisions to rational objectivity, is acting like a court of law, not a human being. His relations are with the abstract *all*, not the particular *some*. He is correct, but heartless; he is Mr Casaubon in *Middlemarch*, 'bent on fulfilling unimpeachably all requirements' but incapable of family affection.[7]

As Hegel emphasises, the wish to remain abstract, disembodied and ideal—to translate into one's social existence the quality of isolation which properly obtains only in our minds—is a very dangerous wish. Whether the isolationist instinct takes the form (common in the post-Christian West) of hedonistic, despairing selfishness, the form (common in nations benighted by poverty and despotism) of blind fanaticism, or the form (common nowhere anymore but of a piece with these other two) of contemplative asceticism, the impulse in each case is the same: to evade, or even destroy, the concrete reality of society and attain an identity which is abstracted from its messy, uncontrollable influences.* And this

---

* Hegel accurately, if abstrusely, describes the character of the French Revolution, of Al Qa'eda or Pol Pol's Cambodia, or of the cult of Western hedonism:

'this absolute possibility of abstracting from every determination in which I find myself, the flight from every content as a limitation… is negative freedom…. This is the freedom of the void, which is raised to the status of an actual shape and passion. If it remains purely theoretical, it becomes in the religious realm the Hindu fanaticism of pure contemplation; but if it turns to actuality, it becomes in the realm of both politics and religion the fanaticism of destruction, demolishing the whole existing social order, eliminating all individuals regarded as suspect by a given order, and annihilating any organisation which attempts to rise up anew. Only in destroying something does this negative will have a feeling of its own existence. It may well believe that it wills some positive condition, for instance the condition of absolute equality or of universal religious life, but it does not in fact will the positive actuality of this condition, for this at once gives rise to some kind of order, a particularisation both of institutions and of individuals; but it is precisely through the annihilation of particularity and of objective determination that the self-consciousness of this negative freedom arises. Thus, whatever such freedom believes that it wills can in itself be no more than an abstract representation, and its

is precisely what we should not do. We must perform the dialectic. We must leave our negative liberty behind, and enter into the positive liberty of society. Those elements of negative liberty which matter—life, liberty and property—are safely guarded by the state. Our business now is positive.

If the individual man in isolation is the beginning of the social dialectic, the real individual of flesh and blood is its end: the 'real' individual is the product, not the progenitor, of civilisation. For freedom is attained, said Hegel, not by the individual divorcing himself from society but by marrying it. True—what he called 'concrete'—freedom is not 'the freedom of the void'. It is the freedom of 'finding oneself' in society; of 'being with oneself in another'. By my marriage with society I attain my true self, which before was abstract. I am realised, socialised; I whisk aside the veil of ignorance, 'the colourful canvas of the world is before me'; I plunge into it, and find myself 'at home'.[8]

The mysterious dialectic is explained, more eloquently than Hegel ever managed, by Roger Scruton, describing how, in middle age, he found his home among the fraternity of fox-hunters:

> Once it was I who contained the world—a private, bookish world, improvised from ruined dreams. I was the existentialist hero of a drama scripted by myself. I contain the world no longer—I am contained by it. And it is a public, objective, concrete world, whose rules were established without my help and with no knowledge of my existence. I have lost my pride, and gained my composure.[9]

Social justice as membership

This, then, is social justice according to the Right. It is not 'emancipation' or 'equality'. It concerns morality, not moral-

---

actualisation can only be the fury of destruction.' (*Elements of the Philosophy of Right*, 1821.)

ism. It is less concerned with the large issues of democracy and economics, or the correct word of the law, or one's abstract stance on this or that grand issue, than with one's own life, and one's conduct towards others—with one's neighbourliness, in short.

Where the Left imagine social justice to be the realisation of certain abstract ideas—equality and emancipation—the Right see it as a system of naturally occurring and beneficial relationships. Social justice is the fulfilment of the individual's need for positive liberty through social membership.

The principles of equality and emancipation are necessary to social justice, in the sense that equality under the law and individual freedom made the original social contract which enables civilisation to exist. But they simply bracket social justice on either side; they are helpful only if they remain at the margins.

When Tony Blair speaks of his wish to 'rebuild civil society around a new contract between citizen and state', he betrays a misunderstanding of what civil society is.[10] There can only be one 'contract between citizen and state': the old one, between liberty and equality: the social contract itself, by which the individual submits to the rule of law on the condition that the law protects his life, liberty and property equally with everyone else's. Any 'new' contract between citizen and state would be an unnatural one, aggrandising either liberty (by extending further 'rights' to personal self-determination) or equality (by extending the coercive powers of government over more areas of social life) or—most likely—both. Such a contract would necessarily involve damage to that which Mr Blair intended it to 'rebuild': civil society. This is not built by a contract, and certainly not one between citizen and state. It grows through a covenant between free individuals and free institutions.

It is often said that poverty is not absolute but relative— that is, one may still be 'poor' even if one has material security, so long as others are considerably richer—and this is undeniably true. Social justice is certainly absent where inequality is chronic and persistent, and in Britain today it still is. But there are more terrible and immediate travesties of social justice than this. The state of one's local relationships, most obviously with family and neighbours, are a more pressing concern than one's place on the national income scale. The security of the public spaces, the social health of one's community, is of more relevance to social justice than relative income. The most important indicator of poverty or wealth is not so much relative as *relational*; the membership one most often thinks about is not the national membership, but one's membership in a more mixed and variable set of associations—associations particular to *you*.

Love and the law

Social justice is relational, but it is not purely parochial. It exists in the health of local relationships, but it has a transcendent quality too. To put it at its plainest, social justice is *love*. This is the most profound and elemental instance of the dialectic at work. The thesis first: the individual retains his essential autonomy, what Hegel called his 'abstract right', in those respects where he can be abstractly conceived, i.e. in the respects belonging to a state of isolation, where his life, liberty and property, and nothing else, are safe from the depredations of others. These freedoms are *retained* in society. But the individual *attains* freedom too, freedom of the positive sort, by submitting to the antithesis and making his home in a society which understands him. 'Love is the most immense contradiction', said Hegel. It is the process by which 'I find myself in another person... I gain recognition [or 'identity'] in this person, who in turn gains recognition in me.' Even in marriage, even in love, the individual remains himself, and has his rights; but he is at his best, happiest, and most complete when he is 'in the other'.[11]

It is, perhaps, an indicator of the retreat of the social sphere that love is now purely thought of as subsisting within a family ('loved ones') or a nation ('love of country'), but rarely within a neighbourhood. For love is also the ethic governing a healthy social order.

'Love does no harm to neighbours,' said St Paul, 'therefore love is the fulfilment of the law.'[12] The distinction is confirmed by Jewish tradition, which sees a transcendent ethic behind the quotidian law: as Jonathan Sacks explains, Jews distinguish between *mishpat*, the strict procedural rule of law, and *tzedekah*, the honouring of social justice through concern for wider society.[13] The Greeks had a word for it too: *dikaiosunē*. This is the 'virtue' or 'sense' of justice, and is distinct from *dikē*, which is the concrete application of that virtue in the legal or administrative system. 'A sense of justice (*dikaiosunē*),' says Aristotle, 'decides what is just (*dikē*).'[14] *Dikaiosunē* is the principle which stands behind the law, which the law aims to realise.

The English legal tradition is a relationship between *dikē* and *dikaiosunē*, between *mishpat* and *tzedekah*. Put another way, the law is subject to precisely the same dialectic process as that undergone by the individual. There is more to the law than negative liberty in its pure form, enshrining the abstract rights of the man in isolation. If our law comprised merely the injunction on all to respect the life, liberty and property of others, it could be expressed in that short statement—whereas it runs to countless volumes. The law has acquired flesh: the negative abstractions of Magna Carta and the Bill of Rights have attained meaning through their application in precedent and case law. Indeed, the pure terms of these written monuments to liberty are themselves simply codifications of the principles of law, teased out by the customs and conventions of English society: they *recognise*, they do not create, the principles they declare. Resting on the fundamental principle of English freedom, abstractly proclaimed in statute and charter, the common law operates through the case-by-case outworking of that principle in specific instances; it responds to, as it shapes, the changing social mores. The end result, still unfolding, is 'real' liberty, neither wholly theoretical nor wholly contingent: the liberty of the individual, made meaningful and particular—made to suit the Englishman.

The bare individualism of the law is further softened by two developments of the centuries. The first is the assumption that 'equity justice'—*aequitas*, 'fairness'—has precedence over *strictum jus*, the literal application of the law. When a literal obedience to precedent or statute would be plainly unjust, equity prevails. The other development is the evolution of tort law, which strengthens the principle that rights carry responsibilities by the convention of the 'duty of care' which we owe to the innocent stranger.[15]

Equity justice and tort law are attempts to bridge the gap between the social contract and social justice. But they do not quite make it. The law remains the law, for it is statutory, essentially contractual. The thesis state is challenged and reformed by the antithesis society, but it remains statist. The law is, thankfully, ringed by its own limitations, incapable of moving beyond the boundaries of *nulla poena sine lege*: where there is no law there is no transgression, or what is not prohibited is permitted. And yet our concern does not stop at those boundaries. Not everything that 'is permitted', said St Paul: 'is beneficial'.[16] How do we encourage behaviour which is not merely legal, but actually beneficial?

Social Authority

If permitted behaviour is *allowed*, negatively, by *coercion* against its opposite, beneficial behaviour is *encouraged*, positively, by *authority*. The distinction is observed by Locke:

> It is one thing to owe honour, respect, gratitude and assistance: another to require obedience and submission…. These two powers, paternal and political, are… perfectly distinct and separate.[17]

Authority is the function of society. Statists and liberals are both hostile to social authority, though they disagree over their response to it. To the statist, authority is irrelevant: only coercion counts. 'Words and breath,' said Hobbes, 'have no force to oblige, contain, constrain, or protect any man'; the only effective stimulus is 'the public sword'.[18] To the liberal, by contrast, authority does have force, but it is a malign one. 'Society can and does execute its own mandates', acknowledged John Stuart Mill, adding that these are even more effective than the official injunctions of the state: they 'penetrat[e] much more deeply into the details of life, and enslav[e] the soul itself'.[19] Such mandates, he thought, should be disobeyed.

New Labour contrives to agree with both Hobbes and Mill. The egalitarian, statist strain in the Left dialectic regards coercion—the executive orders of the government—as the only real fount of legitimacy; the liberal strain sees its duty to 'emancipate' the individual from the mandates of society. To the conservative, however, both Hobbes and Mill are wrong. *Contra* Hobbes, social authority is usually efficacious; and *contra* Mill, it should usually be obeyed. Neither the *you must* of the statist, nor the *I shall* of the liberal, but the *we should* of the conservative, is best.

What is social authority? It is the set of encouragements and admonitions which operates in settled neighbourhoods and among people who trust each other. It connects deeply and truly with the public. It is always up to date because it is the authority of real people, not the abstraction of government edict or of the solitary individual will. It does not require the stamp of the state to give it life. It is not political but social. It is not international, but national and even local. It is not sovereign and concentrated, but influential and dispersed. It is not coercive but persuasive. It is not always strong and clear, but often obscure and weak. It is not uniform but variable and patchy. It is not inflexible and unrelenting, but capable of a thousand revisions and remissions: it adapts not to instructions from above but to the circumstances it encounters on the ground. It is not ordained, but inherited. Its edicts conquer the heart before they convert the head.

Social authority should not be confused with top-down authoritarianism, which is either merely statism exercised in the name of conservatism—the error of Franco or Pinochet— or social authority which has no element of liberalism in it. In the British context, it should not be confused with the values of the 1950s. Social authority then was homogenous and hegemonic. The core was too hard and the margin was too thin: people outside suffered the exclusion of snobbery and people inside were stunted by conformity.[†]

[†] In quoting Mill disapprovingly throughout this essay I am conscious of taking him out of his historical context—the same error, mind, which is committed by those who quote Mill approvingly, to justify their iconoclasm in a time when the icons are already in smithereens. In the 1850s Mill was asserting the need for more liberal individualism in a culture where social authority was too overbearing—and the same might perhaps apply with almost as much force to the 1950s:

'In our times, from the highest class of society down to the lowest, everyone lives as under the eye of a hostile and dreaded censorship. Not only in what concerns others, but in what concerns

We must move with the dialectic. Britain's traditional social authority has been thoroughly discombobulated by the diversity of society since the 1960s. We have shifted, as the sociologists say, from an age of 'deference' to one of 'reference'. We are not happy with hierarchical social forms, but we do want social forms: we do want a culture which, in its multitudinous memberships, its understandings and allegiances, holds us together. 'Take but degree away' said Shakespeare's Ulysses, and 'discord follows'.[20] The 'degree' need not be (as it was for Ulysses) vertical. What matters is *relation*—being at once differentiated yet tied together. Hierarchical structures, the degrees of rank, status, and taste, achieved this, but they are no longer necessary. The social authority we want to see emerging is a more relaxed, but equally decent 'relationism' to that of the past—less

---

only themselves, the individual or the family do not ask themselves—what do I prefer? or, what would suit my character and disposition? or, what would allow the best and highest in me to have fair play, and enable it to grow and thrive? They ask themselves, what is suitable to my position? What is usually done by persons of my station and pecuniary circumstances? Or (worse still) what is usually done by persons of a station and circumstances superior to mine? I do not mean that they choose what is customary, in preference to what suits their own inclinations. It does not occur to them to have any inclination, except for what is customary. Thus the mind itself is bowed to the yoke: even in what people do for pleasure, conformity is the first thing thought of; they like in crowds; they exercise choice only among things commonly done: peculiarity of taste, eccentricity of conduct, are shunned equally with crimes: until by dint of not following their own nature, they have no nature to follow: their human capacities are withered and starved: they become incapable of any strong wishes or native pleasures, and are generally without either opinions or feelings of home growth, or properly their own. Now is this, or is it not, the desirable condition of human nature?'. (Mill, *On Liberty*, 1859.)

respectable, perhaps, but equally responsible. Locke, quoted above, said 'paternal': we say 'fraternal'.

The difference between the authoritarianism of Franco or Pinochet and the social authority of British conservatism is apparent in the fact that social authority creates the space in which freedom—real freedom, not the freedom of caprice and iconoclasm—can thrive. The great liberal economist Friedrich von Hayek eloquently articulates the natural relation of authority and liberty. 'Voluntary conformity may be a condition of a beneficial working of freedom', he says:

> It is indeed a truth, which all the great apostles of freedom outside the rationalistic school have never tired of emphasising, that freedom has never worked without deeply ingrained moral beliefs and that coercion can be reduced to a minimum only where individuals can be expected as a rule to conform voluntarily to certain principles.[21]

Social authority is not an instrument of, but a bulwark against, the excesses of power, and far from restricting freedom it protects and enhances it. As even Mill, with the peculiar blindness to cause and effect which marks his excessive brand of liberalism, observed, 'in England... though the yoke of opinion is perhaps heavier, that of law is lighter, than in most other countries of Europe.'[22]

That is how it should be. The condition helps explain the tremendous economic prosperity and civil peace which has long characterised our country. For in assisting liberty, authority partakes of it too: conformity is, as Hayek said, 'voluntary'. Dissent is not illegal, merely frowned upon—permitted, but not encouraged. And so, by those prepared to withstand the frowns, incremental alterations may be made. Hayek again:

> the existence of individuals and groups observing partially different rules provides the opportunity for the selection of the more effective ones [by others].[23]

Anti-authority

The Left, albeit obliquely, recognises the need for social authority. Indeed much of the language of New Labour is designed to capture from the Right the ideas of authority, and the sense of belonging, community and safety inherent in the notion of 'society'.

Conservatives talk, dustily, of 'home', 'neighbourhood', 'respectability' and 'duty'; New Labour talk of 'social cohesion', 'community', 'civic spirit' and 'civic engagement'. What is happening is that the Left is reaching for new ways of describing those feelings and forces which, over fifty years, their own policies and prejudices have successively degraded. Indeed, it is precisely *because* the egalitarian and libertarian forces in politics have been so effective, that the need is now felt for that quality—call it belonging and the sense of home, or call it social cohesion and the civic spirit— which is sadly lacking in some areas. And the central, triumphant feat of dialectical cunning performed by the Left, quite honestly and ingenuously, is their loading of the blame for the disappearance of civic spirit onto the Right. They believe that freedom and individual self-responsibility is at fault for the loss of social values, rather than the steady legal, fiscal and cultural erosion of benevolent social institutions by the state. Naturally, this analysis justifies the *further* extension of the state into the lives of families and communities, an extension legitimated and strengthened by the appeal to conservative values, by the language of 'engagement' and 'partnership' between society and the state.

The point was articulated fiercely and righteously by Michael Oakeshott in 1962:

> Moral ideals are a sediment; they have significance only so long as they are suspended in a religious or social tradition, so long as they belong to a religious or social way of life. The predicament of our

time is that the rationalists have been at work so long on their project of drawing off the liquid in which our moral ideals were suspended (and pouring it away as worthless) that we are left only with the dry and gritty residue which chokes us as we try to take it down. First, we do our best to destroy parental authority (because of its alleged abuse), then we sentimentally deplore the scarcity of 'good homes', and we end by creating substitutes which complete the work of destruction. And it is for this reason that, among much else that is corrupt and unhealthy, we have the spectacle of a set of sanctimonious, rationalist politicians, preaching an ideology of unselfishness and social service to a population in which they and their predecessors have done their best to destroy the only living root of moral behaviour...[24]

The culture of respectability which we have been at such pains to erode once operated by example. As an individual you knew your own weakness, but as a social being you knew what you had to live up to—and by the example of others you knew you could do it. Today, we have de-legitimised morality, and replaced it with the thin and distant abstractions of moralism. The result is that there is no external principle to encourage us, but merely the power of our own good sense, which was never strong. Once, the individual was known to be fallible—indeed, fallen—but society could set him upright; now, the individual is supposed to be perfect, and to stand unaided, while society does all it can to destabilise him. Previously our personal weakness railed against, but submitted to, the standards expected by bourgeois culture; today our personal virtue is expected to stand alone against the debilitating influence of our surroundings. And to add irony to injury, all the messages propagated by culture—advertising, most of all, and its dependant industries, TV, film and popular magazines—communicate the expectation that, adrift in this sea of moral disaster, kept afloat only by our own frantic efforts, we must be not only personally healthy, wealthy, good-looking and sexually carefree, but must also enjoy loving family and neighbourly relationships. No wonder so many individuals give up the struggle, and families sink.

The loss of benign social authority is the root of our discontents. In its place we have a malign anti-authority: society has been subverted, and propagates not the culture of respectability but the twin errors of socialism and ultra-liberalism. We are in the grip of an official mindset which seeks not to uphold and give expression to, but to clamp down on and alter, the common culture of the country. For under the terms of anti-authority, the prevailing culture is one in which no culture is 'valid' — except this one, of course. It is an irony of very easy deconstruction that the culture which denies the validity of culture, on the grounds that all culture is social control, must itself exercise a very strong social control if it is to survive and prevail. Hence 'political correctness', which is, in its increasingly common form, not a revival of good manners and decency, but an enforced orthodoxy and a wilful refusal to face facts or make moral distinctions.

The Left's attempt to claim the notion of authority, albeit repackaged in value-free language, is a recognition of the limits of the egalitarian and liberal principles. Professor Giddens accepts that more is needed than 'equality' and 'emancipation'. There is also, he says, a need for 'what I have called... life politics', which concerns not collectivism or individualism, but 'choice, identity [and] mutuality'. More precisely, he says, we are concerned with the question of 'how to recreate social solidarity'.

Which is to say, 'life politics' concerns the sphere of fraternity, of authority, of society. Yet Professor Giddens has a different approach to this sphere from that of conservatives: the challenge, he says, is 'how to live without tradition'. His answer is equality and emancipation: a large and active state in which 'strong emphasis has to be given to cosmopolitan values'.

We have in New Labour a positive celebration of the retreat from social authority, albeit disguised as its 'recasting'. Professor Giddens states that in the age of the 'new individualism' authority should be 'democratic'. As he argues, there can be:

> no authority without democracy.... In a society where tradition and custom are losing their hold, the only route to the establishing of authority is via democracy. The new individualism doesn't inevitably corrode authority, but demands that it be recast on an active or participatory basis.[25]

It is certainly true that authority should be 'active or participatory'; and that 'democracy'—most of all local and direct democracy—is crucial to this. And yet the 'tradition and custom' which Professor Giddens deprecates is, of course, the very essence of the 'active or participatory' authority he celebrates. As conservatives have always argued, there can be nothing more 'democratic' than tradition. It is the method by which we enfranchise our ancestors: the authority which emerges is the cumulative, collective vote of all generations past and present. Indeed the very 'authority' the professor wishes for—his own socio-moral outlook, that is—is itself the evolved product of the 'tradition and custom' which he complacently notes the passing of. Our ancestors, he implies, were put-upon and misguided, the victims of indoctrination and false consciousness, whereas he himself, and those who think like him, are alone capable of intellectual self-determination. But the enlightened liberal world-view did not spring fully-formed from the mind of Locke, or Mill, or Giddens. It is the product of generations. The professor plucks the flower and scorns the root; he spurns the soil for the meretricious cultivation.

Good for him: he holds the flower. But his doctrines are poisoning the roots on which lesser beings depend. For while people at the top—with their large incomes and their assured social status, their excellent education and their wide support networks of family and friends and colleagues, their safe streets and their sense of belonging to the official culture of the country—while they themselves can get along in a world with all the icons smashed, others cannot. In a Britain 'debunked' of all its 'myths' and lacking the 'patriarchal' influence of authority, only the rich can prosper—the rest are left to construct their own approximations to authority, with disastrous effects.

For if anti-authority is paramount at the top of our national life, it is also endemic at the bottom. Many clients of the state, deriving their income and receiving their moral messages from the government, are as cut off from the culture of social authority as their patrons. Denied the beneficent effect of independent social institutions, members only of the local social security office and, if children, of a local gang, they lack not just the institutional supports which might hold them up in the turbulence of their lives, but also that internal sense of worth and confidence which should help them to stand unaided. The *haute bourgeoisie*, in appeasing their own guilt through morale-sapping welfarism, have accomplished the ruin of the state's dependents as surely as they have hollowed out their own sense of purpose. The state and its culture—welfarism and the shibboleths of Left-liberalism—have enervated poor and rich alike.

Yet many millions, the suburban recusants, still adhere to the proscribed articles of social authority, articles which the courtiers and the intellectuals are estranged by choice, and the poor by circumstance. Anti-authority, as a positive, celebrated culture, has not penetrated much deeper than the government (and the institutions which orbit it: the public services, local government, the universities, the arts and the London broadcast media) and the welfare-supported classes. The decree that the emperor is clothed is upheld only where the state and its satellites hold sway.

Given this hegemony over the institutions at the top of our national life, the alternative, real, original social authority can be celebrated only unofficially, almost in secret: in the pubs and clubs and houses where the ambit of anti-authority does not reach. The effect is that the public conversation is stilted, stunted by obeisance to the dogmas of the Left. 'The genuinely popular culture of England', said Orwell, 'is something that goes on beneath the surface, unofficially and more or less frowned on by the authorities.'[26] Only private conversation flourishes, and only in the places where private institutions—pub and club and home—are strong enough to sustain it.

Civil society

'Authority', said Enoch Powell, 'is immanent in institutions.'[27] But which institutions? The state has acquired ownership and control of many: schools, hospitals, welfare agencies and local government. And the state is essentially coercive. For it has at its disposal the use of compulsion, and the law which legitimises and directs that use: consequently all its activities are coloured by compulsion. When it steps into the sphere of social relations—and the functions of welfare, education and healthcare are essentially social—it is coercion, not authority, equality, not fraternity, which is applied.

The confusion of coercion with authority, equality with fraternity, is apparent in our public services. As Hayek says, there are really two sorts of law which operate in our country. One, the traditional, liberal sort, addresses itself to the individual, and seeks to protect his rights to life, liberty and property. The other sort are not really laws at all:

> but rather instructions issued by the state to its servants concerning the manner in which they are to direct the apparatus of government and the means which are at their disposal.

The 'means at their disposal' are the schools, hospitals and welfare agents which the government has nationalised or established. And as Hayek says, although their functions:

> are presented as mere service activities, they really constitute an exercise of the coercive powers of government and rest on its claiming exclusive rights in certain fields.[28]

The key to Hegel's dialectic is the principle that the relationship of thesis to antithesis must be 'based on truth'. Not any social identification will do: the one must relate to the other in a meaningful way—in a way which is, as he put it, 'ethical'.[29] But one cannot have an 'ethical', only an official relationship with the state. An attempt at an 'ethical' relationship with the state would not be 'based on truth' but on a falsehood—namely that officialdom, anonymous and devoid of humanity, can be a meaningful element of a person's identity. The state is *thetic* in its operations, sharing with the individual himself the qualities of idealism, unity and abstraction. Acting in the world, it is blind, bland and pitiless: in the position of the antithesis it will not (as the antithesis should) accommodate and 'realise' the individual, but crush him; it will exact not loyalty and affection but subservience and conformity.

A truly 'ethical' relationship is had with another order of institution altogether. Whereas the state is mechanical, cold and indifferent to the humans it rules over, ethical institutions respond to the loyalty which is shown them. They swell and shift with the addition of another human member; they are composed of the organic matter of their constituents. Membership is not negative and acquisitive, the taking of things into your own embrace, but positive and generous, the giving of yourself into the embrace of others. It simultaneously humbles and exalts. It humbles you by showing that you are smaller than something—the group and its history—and that your personal interests are secondary to those of the collective; but it exalts you too, by conferring the privilege of belonging, and granting you your share of the general glory. This is perfect safety.

Ethical institutions compose 'civil society'. The phrase has a long history. It was originally used to mean organised society, as distinct from the state of nature: a community subject to law and with a recognisable polity. Its root is embarrassing for my argument, which requires the terms 'civil' and 'political' to have different spheres, those of society and the state respectively: in fact, Hayek reminds us, the two terms derive respectively from Latin and Greek words with the same meaning.[30] To the ancients, there was no difference between the spheres—the term from which we derive 'republic', for instance, meant both state and society. Yet the common root of 'civil' and 'political' illustrates the feature of the classical world to which Hegel attributed its decline: the absence of an 'ethical life', of institutions to which individuals could relate other than the state.

It is a central tenet of modern Western civilisation that state and society—the civil and the political, fraternity and equality—are distinct. The distinction was observed, naturally enough, by Hegel, who translated the German word *Bürger* into French not as *citoyen* but as *bourgeois*. One's local and particular identity, he implied, was distinct from one's recognition by the state.

The term bourgeois has further connotations than simply 'townsman'. It means 'capitalist' too. Civil society, in Hegel's scheme, is the sphere of individual choice and association outside the home, and that sphere includes the system of private property, or the market economy. The Left (like the ancients) conflate state and society, and oppose the conflation of the two to the unfettered liberalism of the market. As Professor Giddens puts it, 'government... and communities' must together supply the wants of 'the market'. For, he says, 'markets cannot even function without a social and ethical framework—which they themselves cannot provide'. Therefore 'ethical standards... have to be brought in from outside—from a public ethics, guaranteed in law'.[31]

As this illustrates, a dangerous consequence of the Left's colonising of the discourse—their successful annexation of the language of social engagement—has been the rebranding of the term 'civil society' to exclude commercial enterprise. The phrase is now almost coterminous with the 'voluntary sector', which is itself a somewhat ill-defined term. It cannot mean 'unpaid', because people who work for pay also do so voluntarily; and anyway, most people working in what is called the 'voluntary sector' *are* paid. The term really means the 'non-profit' sector. But again, what does this mean? 'Non-profits' aim to break even, presumably, and even to generate a surplus: it seems odd to build a categorical and moral distinction on whether that surplus is ploughed back into the business, or devoted to the people (the owners) whose initial—risky—investment made the enterprise possible. Indeed, it is perverse to suggest an enterprise is more moral because it consumes its own surplus, instead of distributing it throughout the economy to fertilise other enterprises.

So while the Left (*vide* Giddens) forcibly unites 'government... and communities' against 'the market', the Right divides civil society from the state and allies it with the individual; 'communities' are wrested from 'government' and married with 'the market'.

The relation of market with society, liberty with fraternity, challenges the assumption that commercial enterprise is essentially selfish, individualistic and destructive of social life. To be sure, a business (or an individual) can be such, but only if it (or he) refuses to perform the dialectic operation. If *autonomy* refuses to suffer the socialising effects of *authority*, it will approach the Left's caricature. But a business which is properly accommodated among the diverse variety of other institutions (commercial and otherwise) which make up civil society is not harmful, but 'at home' there.

As management theory now emphasises, and as classical economics has long recognised, an individual, a business or an economy does not prosper on account of liberty pure and simple—on the selfish, aggrandising liberty of the man in isolation. A business depends on the qualities of trust and sympathy, on common understanding as well as common avarice. Indeed, as Adam Smith wrote two hundred years before the 'iterated prisoner's dilemma' was coined to demonstrate the same point, 'whenever dealings are frequent, a man does not expect to gain so much by any one contract as by probity and punctuality in the whole'.‡ [32]

---

‡   The 'prisoner's dilemma', in which two felons, kept in different cells, fail to gain the shortest sentences for themselves because each attempts to stitch the other up, showed that when individuals are separated from each other individual benefit is lost because short-sighted self-interest damages social co-operation. The dilemma was resolved by Robert Axelrod, who pointed out that the felons made the wrong move because the choice only came before them once; if the scenario were 'iterated' repeatedly over time, so that the felons recognised that generosity has reciprocal benefits, they would develop trust, and even without direct communication would arrive at a mutually advantageous agreement.

Similarly, the creation of wealth is not the sole motivating purpose of a successful and sustainable enterprise. The maximisation of individual advantage—the extreme of liberalism—is deficient, for it fails to provide the fulfilment which is achieved through membership of, and allegiance to, an institution. Hegel famously argued that the slave could be more 'free' than the master, for the slave is contextualised, subject to circumstance, and *related* to his fellows even if only through their common bondage. Even though he lacks liberty, one of the three rights of negative freedom (even slaves, in ancient Rome, had the right to life and property), he has more positive freedom than his master, whose wealth makes him independent, and so un-related to others. The slave is *realised*, and the master is not.

This is stretching things a little. For without the negative liberty which underpins one's autonomy, all the positive liberty of belonging and acceptance counts for nought; it becomes, indeed, the stifling opposite of liberty. Authority requires autonomy, not coercion, as its ally. The natural alliance, the consanguinity of society and the individual, is evident in the qualities shared by both 'voluntary' and commercial organisations: the freedom, independence and initiative, the competition and entrepreneurial spirit apparent in business, is apparent also in a wide range of private institutions whose purpose is not commercial. Charities, clubs, churches, trades unions, friendly societies, co-operatives, teams, parties and protest groups all share the vitality and vigour of the commercial world; or they should.

The same consanguinity is evident in the users or clients of the organisation. A defining feature of the institutions of civil society—commercial or non-profit—is that the individual associates with them voluntarily. And yet, in the range of institutions and associations which make up civil society there is a very important irony—or more accurately, a very important illustration of the Hegelian dialectic. The range implies *choice*: the variety of available social groups caters to the great diversity of the population: every individual can find his 'home' somewhere. And the irony consists in this: that the end, the whole purpose of this liberalised marketplace is to enable each individual to escape from the marketplace and the tyranny of choice. In dialectic process he moves from freedom to belonging, from independence to membership. By and large, and commendably, most people choose to stay where they are—to 'join' the institution (the town, the club, the culture) closest to home—though the choice is always before them to move away and join others. The great liberty, as Hegel explained, is the liberty *not* to exercise your liberty: the free decision to stay put.

It is this paradox which helps resolve one of the most difficult controversies in current public policy: the question of 'choice' in healthcare and education. It is often pointed out that most people do not want to have to 'choose' which school or hospital to use: they want a good local institution which everyone uses. Yet it is equally obvious that many 'local' schools and hospitals are not 'good' enough.

The mistake the system makes is a dialectic one: it fails to cede any freedom to the institution or to its users. It fails to accept that, given *liberty*, there could be any *authority* in the arrangement. A system lacking the coercion of *equality*, it is thought, will be one of *liberty* only, without *fraternity*— autonomy without social responsibility, solidarity or morality. Take away coercion, and there shall be the Hobbesian chaos, the ghettoisation of rich and poor and the exploitation of advantage by the strong.

The counter-argument was succinctly put by the nineteenth-century anarchist Frédéric Bastiat:

When under the pretext of fraternity the legal code imposes mutual sacrifices on citizens, human nature is not thereby abrogated. Everyone will then direct his efforts toward contributing little to, and taking much from, the common fund of sacrifices. Now, is it the most unfortunate who gains from this struggle? Certainly not, but rather the most influential and calculating.[33]

The Right, armed with the dialectic relationship of freedom and authority, sees things as they are. It is only by giving *liberty* to an institution and its users that *fraternity* will develop there; the goal of 'good, local' schools and hospitals will only be gained by ceding power to the people who run and use them. 'Choice', then, is not the obligation to shop around, but the guarantee of peace of mind. The Right does not envisage the ceaseless exercise of consumer choice in the matter of health and education, but a system which, more than any other, will ensure high standards across the board, and the consequent 'choice' to stay at home.

The preference for particular freedom over statutory direction applies as well to communities as to individuals. The point was observed, long before the welfare state, by De Tocqueville, who distinguished between 'political' and 'administrative' functions: one concerns 'interests... common to all parts of the nation'; the other 'interests of special concern to certain parts of the nation'. De Tocqueville attributed the success of English and American society in his day to their high degree of 'political' and their low degree of 'administrative' centralisation; the difficulties experienced by France were due to her having a high degree of both; while Germany's problems were because of her low degree of both.[34] Germany has long since gone over to the French way of doing things—and Britain is following. Even in the nineteenth century, Disraeli was complaining that the state was degraded into 'fulfilling municipal rather than imperial offices... performing functions... which many in their civic spheres believe they could accomplish'.[35] Today, there are no imperial offices to fulfil; there are municipal ones aplenty, and the state fulfils them all. For all that New Labour pretends a love of localism, and cites its support of devolved government in Scotland and Wales and the English 'regions', the reality of the last nine years has been of steady centralisation. For as Anthony Giddens candidly admits, 'devolution can lead to fragmentation if not matched with a transfer of power "upwards"'.[36]

Family and nation

At either end of society, as it were—at the most private end closest to the individual, and the most public end closest to the state—are two social forms which frame between them all the other private institutions and associations of civil society. These are the family and the nation. It is debatable whether they can properly be classified with the associations of 'society' at all. To Hegel family and nation did not represent elements of society, distinct from individual and state on either side: to him family and individual were inseparable, as were nation and state. This is a feature, perhaps, of his time and place, and doubtless of his temperament. Hegel was sufficiently paternalist, both privately and politically, to contract the existence of wife and children into the existence of the father, who was by dialectic process not so much an individual as a whole family incarnated in a single person—and similarly, to contract the nation as a whole into the person and office of the monarch.

The English tradition, however, has enough liberalism in it to defend the position of the individual, independent in some sense even of his family, and to insist on the distinction between society as a whole (the nation) and the organs of the government. Family and nation are well described in Catholic social teaching as the two 'natural societies'.[37] They should be classified with society, for they share the antithetic, Aristotelian, 'realising' qualities which transcend the chill Platonic formality of individual and state. They are not abstract and withdrawn, but vividly real and engaged. They are *ethical*: they are not, as the state is, indifferent to us, their component members; rather, they accommodate, figure-forth, and realise us.

But they differ from the other institutions of society in one crucial respect: our membership of them is involuntary. I have argued that the central irony of social associations is that while they offer us refuge from the tyranny of individual choice, we are required to choose the associations to belong to. The same cannot be said for one's family and nation. You can leave them physically, you can forsake them emotionally, but you remain a life member simply by virtue of your birth (adoption by another family, or naturalisation in another country, are artificial—though no less real for that—simulations of this natural fact). Many countries and cultures insist on a formal rite of passage, marking a conscious act of will by which the young adult accedes to the privileges of citizenship (in ancient Greece, Aristotle reminds us, this included participation in a 'tragedy' or drama). But such rites are simply the official representation of something already real: national membership, as involuntary as one's family membership.

Here we see another important instance of the difference between Left and Right. The Left implies that one's national and family memberships are of the same order as one's memberships in society more generally; that they are objects of choice, capable of easy entrance and easy exit. Indeed, to the Left, family and nation are perhaps the institutions which the individual needs 'emancipating' from most—both patriarchy and patriotism being unfashionable on the Left. Hence their support for sexual permissiveness and innovative family formation; and hence their habit of traducing British history and lowering the qualifications for British citizenship.

The Right, by contrast, recognises that family and nation are integral to us all. Rather than trying to emancipate us from them, the Right seeks to prevent damage being done to family and nation, in the knowledge of the disaster such damage brings individually and collectively. In the Introduction, I said that government should take care to maintain the walls around the national home and the family home, ensuring national defence and national sovereignty, and protecting the householder from burglars. There is another, one might say an internal, act of protection which the government is responsible for in respect of these institutions: to maintain not only their walls, but their constitutions.

Family

It is widely asserted that the 'traditional' family is in irreversible decline. This is at once to state the obvious and to misunderstand the nature of families themselves. The family referred to—father working, mother cooking, two or three children at school, all living together but largely cut off (often literally: 'detached') from neighbourhood and wider family—is a 'tradition' of only the last hundred or so years. It is a product, first, of industrialisation which broke up the large rural family-community, with its own little internal economy and welfare system, and created in its place the small 'nuclear' family entirely dependent on the man's weekly wage; and second, of the welfare state which emerged in response to these developments and reinforced them, coming to act variously as traditional father (providing income) and traditional mother (providing education, healthcare and childcare). The first dislocation, caused by the move from country to town, was in some sense meliorated by the emergence of sickness clubs and friendly societies, the institutions of the urban poor which provided families with the wider support system that village and kinship group had provided before. But the second development, the welfare state, put paid to such associations, and the story of the inner city in the second half of the twentieth century is one of social breakdown more pronounced than in the far more materially deprived slums of pre-war Manchester or London.

The decline of this 'traditional', but in fact very modern, family model is a sign of its inefficacy. In Hegelian terms, just as the individual is only 'realised' by being socialised in a family, so the nuclear family cannot comfortably exist independently of the wider community, including the network of aunts and cousins and in-laws and old folk which sustain the difficult job of father and mother.

But in many pockets the inner cities, the Hegelian sublation or *Aufhebung* has been absolute, in that the thesis— the nuclear family—has disappeared altogether into a most messy antithesis: what its apologists are pleased to call the 'reconstituted' or 'blended' family, comprising not only grandparents and neighbours but also step-siblings and half-siblings, 'baby mothers' and 'baby fathers' (the slang for separated co-parents).

Total sublation, where the thesis is not realised but obliterated, occurs when the thesis lacks *coherence*, the structural integrity which holds it together in the jostling of the dialectic process. The thesis individual, in his translation into society, retains coherence and integrity because his essential attributes—his rights to life, liberty and property— are protected in the social contract. A similar operation is necessary for the nuclear family. It, too, requires civil recognition and protection to keep it safe in wider society. And that is what marriage is for.

It is often thought that marriage is a private affair, concerning only the principals: that it simply represents a formal declaration of love and mutual support. In fact marriage is about more than the two people who perform the ceremony—as the ceremony itself indicates. Those vows are of an entirely different quality to the couple's whispered promises of everlasting love: they are public. They say, paradoxically, just at the very moment that two become one and pledge their lives to each other, that they will live for the sake of society as a whole. If love is the process by which the individual 'gains recognition', by which he becomes 'with [him]self in an other', then marriage is the same process performed by the pair of lovers facing the wider world. By promising to look after each other, the couple are promising to look after society; and society responds by awarding the couple the status of joint membership. The two-in-one person, the single human unit which is the married couple, is accorded public recognition and civil privileges because it identifies its own interest and identity with that of society at large. As Hegel says, marriage is 'essentially an ethical relationship'.[38]

Of course, the dialectic is more immediate and obvious than this: it is vigorously incarnate; it has what used to be called 'issue'. As two people are united into a single unit they produce a third person. And parental responsibility for children is of key concern to those outside the family; a commitment on the part of the adults to control and care for the child is a step deserving not only the highest social approbation, but statutory recognition by the government.

It is an article of ultra-liberalism that the state has no place in family life—that for the government even to recognise marriage in the legal or fiscal system is an unwarranted step into the sphere of private relations. But the irony of statutory recognition of marriage is that it actually helps keep the state away from families. The state cannot be 'neutral' towards families—unless it is entirely indifferent to them, and makes no tax or welfare calculations on the basis of the individual's family circumstance at all. For not only do intact families tend to rely less on state support, but even those families that do need help suffer less intrusion if the parents are married. Marriage is a liberal institution.

The illiberalism of the 'non-judgmental' approach to family structure is apparent in those places which have gone furthest along it. In Sweden it was decided that cohabiting couples should have the same benefit and legal entitlements as married ones. But the very nature of cohabitation is its imprecision. The result of this apparently liberal concession is that the most minute and intrusive investigations are required into the exact circumstances and relationships of the couples in question in order to prevent people cheating the system. In its mission of charity the state enters the very bedroom of the couple, to check that they are doing what they say they are doing. With married couples, of course, no such visit is necessary: the sight of a piece of paper, duly sanctified by society and the civil authorities, is enough: the bedroom door stays closed to the state.

Of course, the fact that one element of family life is better than its absence does not make the policy-maker's job any easier. Indeed, it sets up an invidious difficulty. To encourage, through financial rewards, the better option is to punish those who do not choose it; those who are, of course, the most vulnerable people in society—especially single mothers. It costs more to raise a child alone than in a couple. To reward marriage is to make life easier for those who, by their own responsible actions, have made life easier for themselves, and to make life harder for those who, often by ill fortune, already have a hard life.

There are two complementary ways in which we can act constructively towards families—ways which reflect the two sides of the Right dialectic. The principle of freedom carries responsibility: the system should reflect the fact that individuals are responsible for their decisions. This responsibility is enforced naturally on women, who bear children and must care for them, at least initially. Men, however, must have their responsibility brought before them. Marriage deserves approbation in the fiscal and legal codes, to change incentives, and make it in men's interests to do the right thing. The opposite of marriage—abandoning mother and child—deserves harsh disapprobation.

The other side of the dialectic is the principle of social membership. So, in addition to state incentives to encourage individual responsibility, families should be supported through the more diffuse, but ultimately more effective medium of society itself. The culture of broken families which afflicts inner cities is the consequence of anti-authority; real, constructive authority must be re-asserted, and reclaim the lost territory. It must do this with kindness and toughness—with high expectation, but unfailing forgiveness. It will do so by social welfare organisations which can be both sterner and kinder than the state, which can impart moral messages and link reward with virtue in a way which the government cannot. Families must be accommodated within an institutional context which is more reliable and supportive than the broken links of the 'blended' family, and more flexible and responsive than the agencies of the state.

Nation

'The state is an association', said Aristotle in the first sentence of *The Politics*. And while this reflects the ancients' lack of what Hegel called an 'ethical life'—while to Aristotle the state entirely comprehends civil society—it is also, in some sense, true today. I said earlier that we cannot have an ethical, only an official relationship with the state. That is so when the state acts in its essential capacity, the capacity of coercion. As the guarantor of the rule of law, and as the monopoly provider of public goods, the state acts officially, not ethically. And yet there is more to the state than this: it acts with authority as well as with coercion. As Burke put it, the state is more than 'a partnership agreement in a trade of pepper and coffee, calico or tobacco'; common government means more, Hegel agrees, than the 'shared use of facilities'.[39]

The authoritative as well as coercive aspects to the state are apparent in the coercive agency itself: the army. The legal and moral basis of the army is its statism: its function is the exercise of violence. It is, quite rightly, entirely in thrall to Whitehall, taking orders both sweepingly general and minutely particular from politicians and officials. It is a strictly hierarchical organisation with clear lines of command from top to bottom; hardly any autonomy is allowed to front-line staff, who must obey orders even at the point of death. Needless to say, there are no trade unions in the army, and no (or very little) appeal to authorities outside. Its workers are marshalled, regimented and made to march in step: their primary function is to do what they are told. The army works so well as an agency of the government because its purpose is truly egalitarian: it concerns *all*, not *one* or *some*; it exists to protect the country as a whole. It is, indeed, so egalitarian that its activity is actually *external* to the country: it works abroad, and round our coasts. It is a singular, unified agent, serving a singular, unified client, the United Kingdom.

And yet there is more to the army than this. It has, in the term Walter Bageot applied to the constitution, a 'dignified' part to play—apparent in soldiers' parade ground dress rather than their combat fatigues. And internally, the army operates as much by authority as by coercion. Its origins are in the private regiments of noblemen, and it works by subdivision into little platoons. *Esprit de corps*, or fraternity, is a more powerful ligament than the abstraction of patriotism or even the fact of discipline: soldiers fight for their unit as much as for their country, as much to support their comrades as to obey their officers.

The same can be said of the police. While crime is defined as a breach of the social contract—impingement on someone's life, liberty or property—and while it is legally the responsibility of the individual, it is nonetheless a social phenomenon, caused by damaged relationships within a family or a community. The criminal, though solely accountable for his actions, is rarely an isolated individual in practice. There is, as we say, a criminal 'fraternity', itself a tragic inversion of that decent fraternity, the law-abiding community. Both the liberal aspect to crime—the personal responsibility of the individual—and the fraternal aspect— its origins in a broken society—are, or should be, comprehended in the activities and spirit of the police force.

To be sure, as Hobbes put it, 'there be somewhat else required (beside covenant) to make [men's] agreement binding; which is a common power, to keep them in awe.'§40

---

§ Or as T.E. Utley put it, more elegiacally: 'The factors that bind a society together, whether that society be large or small, whether it be a nation or a school, are multifarious and complex, not easily to be defined, nor succinctly to be expressed in any code of conduct or profession of faith, but exerting their cohesive force in subtle and silent ways; yet, strong as these factors may be, which make for the spontaneous co-ordination of will and effort, which is in some measure the mark of all societies, but which is in particular the glorious mark of a free society, they can never be so strong as to dispense with those penal sanctions against the vandal, the thief,

Yet unlike the army (the 'common power' in Hobbes' day), the police are imbued with external authority, to enjoin good behaviour as well as the power to enforce it. They exist to uphold the fraternal values of society as well as the liberal-egalitarian rule of law. 'The police are the public and the public are the police', said Sir Robert Peel in 1829 when he set up the Metropolitan Police Force. Rather than always discharging their official responsibility to the letter, a policeman would preferably practice discretion, enjoining good behaviour by an appeal to social values, not state penalties.

Constitution

This alliance of coercion and authority is evident in our constitution itself. A country's constitution is a dialectic blend of the abstract (theoretical rules imposed by the framers) and the concrete (particular provisions which recognise the traditions and circumstances of the country). Put another way, in Roger Scruton's words, 'power and authority seek each other'—the abstraction of the state (*politiea*) and the concreteness of society (*civitas*) seek each other. 'Their search is the process of politics, while establishment is the condition which their meeting creates.'[41]

In Britain, indeed, our polity has for many years been regulated more by an establishment than by a constitution, so much has the power of the state been tempered by the authority of society. And this establishment—better understood as a set of assumptions about the relations of

---

the sworn enemy of society itself, which are part of the normal apparatus of civil government, and the absence of which signifies not a lofty regard for freedom, as is commonly supposed by 'progressives', but a contemptible indifference to the conditions and limitations that alone make freedom possible.' (Quoted by Tom Utley in the *Daily Telegraph*, 21 April 2006.)

state, society and individual than as a class of powerful people—was so imbued with authority that power deferred to it.

Less so now. In the obvious priorities of policy—crime, healthcare, education, welfare—the Government has failed to translate will into results with much efficacy. But when it comes to the Constitution, they have no such difficulties: no recalcitrant public servants, no institutional inertia, and (perhaps crucially) no suspicious and politicised general public to carp and complain. People are not interested in the Constitution, for the simple reason that they have not needed to be; it is perhaps not stretching the truth to suggest that the majority of the population is not *aware* of the Constitution, as anything more than the reason for their quinquennial visit to the polling station. But that does not mean their affections are not bound up in it; it simply means, rather as the Constitution is itself unwritten, that their affections do not find conscious expression. Attachment to the Constitution is largely negative: it is not so much supported directly, as defended against change simply by the force of lethargy. No party in recent times has ever made the slightest improvement to its popular standing with a promise of constitutional change. But the problem is that this lethargy, though a deep defensive moat prohibiting radical electioneering on constitutional questions, is of no use once the castle has been taken. Inside the citadel of the state Labour have proceeded to rearrange the architecture with hardly a murmur of complaint from outside the walls and hardly a movement of resistance within.

For the British Constitution has no means of its own defence bar the inert instincts of the public. Being unwritten, it is essentially unprotected; the laws and conventions governing our polity are just like all other laws, capable of abrogation by a simple Parliamentary majority: the government of the day can do almost anything it likes. Indeed, Britain actually has less in-built resistance to tyranny than other constitutions, which have experienced it so often. We are used to obeying the law, because, in Mill's words quoted earlier, 'the yoke of law' has been so 'light'; our peace has been sustained not by a written code but by a set of assumptions. The government which decides to ignore those assumptions is very powerful indeed.**

The most pernicious alteration to our Constitution has been a sly and subtle one: the downgrading of Parliament as the seat of sovereignty. This has been achieved precisely because the governing party has had such a large Parliamentary majority, but lacks any respect for the institution which gives it its power. As Ferdinand Mount has written, we are experiencing 'the thinning of the Constitution': the old, established conventions and institutions which hedged the state about have given way to a fetish of formal democracy, whereby the elected government has absolute power for a fixed term—as if the process of deciding our temporary rulers validates their every decision.[42] But as Burke said, laws do not 'derive… authority from their institution, merely and independently of the quality of the subject matter'.[43] Authority is distinct from statute. Yet by the assumption which drives New Labour, not *dikaiosunē*—the unwritten natural law—but *dikē*—the text of statute—is all.

The most important article of the natural law is the debt that a properly liberal order owes to the nation state.

** 'And it is a question whether the much-praised flexibility of the common law, which has been favourable to the evolution of the rule of law so long as that was the accepted political ideal, may not also mean less resistance to the tendencies undermining it, once that vigilance which is needed to keep liberty alive disappears.' (Hayek, *The Constitution of Liberty*, 1960.)

Liberalism emerged as a political creed at the same time — the late seventeenth century in England, the late eighteenth century in Europe and America — as the emergence of nationalism. As Karl Popper, albeit uncomprehendingly, recognised:

> in spite of its internal reactionary and irrational tendencies, modern nationalism, strangely enough, was in its short history before Hegel a revolutionary and liberal creed. By accident it had made its way into the camp of freedom.[44]

That was no accident. As Hayek reminds us, 'etymologically, the Teutonic root of "free" described the position of a protected member of the community'.[45] Liberty applies to a particular jurisdiction: the 'negative' conception of rights is dependent on the 'positive' principle of membership.

To be a 'friend to freedom' in the eighteenth and nineteenth century was to be a 'patriot' — a partisan of national self-government rather than of foreign rule, and of civil and democratic rights rather than of monarchical power. Hegel himself lived through the brief German day between night and night, between 1807 and about 1818, when the nascent German 'nation' united under liberal leadership to throw off the Napoleonic yoke. But the strength which nationalism took from the triumph was requisitioned by the state, and was turned against liberalism, with a series of repressive laws after the Napoleonic danger had passed.

If the nineteenth century in Germany was a time of nationalism without liberalism, with what culmination we know, the tragedy for Europe since 1945 has been the opposite: the adoption of liberalism without nationalism. In the words of the European Convention of Human Rights (ECHR), 'the enjoyment of the rights and freedoms set forth in this Convention shall be secure without discrimination on any grounds such as... national... origin'. By incorporating the ECHR into British Law (the Human Rights Act 1998), New Labour has explicitly severed the link between nationhood and liberty.

Because it has separated liberalism from nationalism, the European Union, for all its apparently 'liberal' rhetoric, poses a serious threat to liberty. The attempt to impose on Britain, for the first time in our history, a written Constitution—written in Brussels, no less, under the supervision of a Frenchman—was not simply an exercise in political duplicity by our elected government. It is an attempt to undo the Revolution Settlement of 1688-89 established under the aegis of John Locke, and revert to the totalitarian conception of statehood urged by Thomas Hobbes. In *Leviathan*, Hobbes had argued that the state must not only be sovereign, but must be omnipotent. Leviathan should have power:

> not only according to the Law he hath formerly made [but also] if there be no Law made, according as he shall judge most to conduce to... [the interests of] the Commonwealth.[46]

This principle underlies the emerging European Union. There was in the draft European Constitution an 'enabling clause'. The EU was to have (and still desires) 'kompetenz-kompetenz'—the competence to decide its own competences (a 'competence', in EU-speak, means a power).

'The owl of Minerva sets her wings only at the gathering of the dusk.'[47] This famous line of Hegel's, showing how one only realises the value of something as it disappears, is dreadfully apposite with regard to the nation state. It is often pointed out that Aristotle, in his immense review of over a hundred independent city states, failed to notice that at the very time of writing these states were on the point of being subsumed by the new regional hegemon, the Macedonian

Empire. The only difference today is that national independence is being surrendered, not vanquished.

Afterword

The Disordered Dialectic

Sometimes there comes a time in the life of nations when old customs are changed, mores destroyed, beliefs shaken, and the prestige of memories has vanished…. Then men see their country only by a weak and doubtful light; their patriotism is not centred on the soil, which in their eyes is just inanimate earth, nor on the customs of their ancestors, which they have been taught to regard as a yoke, nor on religion, which they doubt, nor on the laws, which they do not make, nor on the lawgiver, whom they fear and scorn. So they find their country nowhere, recognising neither its own nor any borrowed features, and they retreat into a narrow and unenlightened egoism.

Alexis de Tocqueville, Democracy in America, 1835-40

Civil society, said Edmund Burke, is in origin 'a voluntary act', yet 'its continuance is under a permanent standing covenant, coexisting with the society; and it attaches upon every individual in that society, without any formal act of his own'.[1]

Historically, the best evidence of the Right dialectic was its invisibility. The distinctions identified in this essay—the distinct notions of individual, state and society—had very little appearance in the reality of Britain. The dialectic was performed so often and so thoroughly than its constituent parts lost their definite aspects: the covenanted relationships of individual, state and society caused them all to merge. Individual and society elided, as a man in tweeds blends into the hillside, so that it was difficult to tell where one's private personality ended and one's identity as a Yorkshireman or an Englishman began. In the same way commercial enterprises, the institutional incarnation of the liberal principles of freedom and property, acquired social aspects, replete with tradition, loyalty and charity; and social enterprises exhibited much of the dynamic and competitive spirit of the free market. The state, too, operated in a covenantal way: what Burke called the 'fond illusions' of the monarchy made 'power gentle and obedience liberal'; the army and the police, the agents of state coercion, exerted also the soft power of authority.

The product of this iterated dialectic, the synthetic blurring of individual, state and society, is itself an ideal— the ideal of England past, fitting to the past sense employed by Roger Scruton throughout his splendid *England: an Elegy* (2000). In modern Britain, the synthesis is coming apart, and the distinctions which before lay buried beneath the accretions of custom are emerging into prominence again. And in doing so they are showing their least lovely aspects. Covenanted relationships are giving way to contractual ones—or none at all. The individual, formerly half-lost in society, is asserting a new and strident independence. Society itself, once infinitely varied but yet cohesive, is becoming roughly divided into large and hostile groups, admitting neither individuality within nor common allegiance between them. We are losing what Orwell called 'the subtle network of compromises by which the nation keeps itself in its familiar shape.'[2]

There are all sorts of reasons for this, economic and cultural, but the principal culprit is the state, which has responded to economic and cultural change in the wrong way. Pursuing the twin ideals of 'emancipation' and 'equality', it has tampered with the 'standing covenant' of society, abandoning its natural protection of the family and the nation and interfering with all the institutions in between. It has forged coercive relationships with the associations—schools, hospitals, welfare agencies and local councils—which minister to families' and neighbourhoods' needs, and so liberated individuals from the ethical connections which once bound them together. The result is a disordering of the dialectic, and a consequent clashing of competing interests—all of which simply emboldens the state to involve itself further in an attempt to repair the damage it has caused. 'Each thing meets in mere oppugnancy', as Shakespeare's Ulysses said, and 'every thing includes itself in power.'[3]

The challenge for our times is to restore the Right dialectic: to nurture once more the native associations, and to build the institutions of local stone, which give meaning to the life of an individual by expressing the habits and wishes of his neighbourhood. The effect will not be—as the Left imagine—a loss of social solidarity, but its revival. Out of freedom, properly tempered by authority, will grow men and women naturally socialised; the diversity of institutions will severally bind us together. And so 'the reciprocal struggle of discordant powers', in Burke's words, will 'draw out the harmony of the universe'.[4]

Notes

Introduction

1 Homily delivered by Pope Benedict XVI at St Peter's Square during his inaugural Mass, 24 April 2005.

2 William Shakespeare, Richard II, Act II Scene 2.

3 Plato, *The Republic*, c. 360 BC.

4 Aristotle, *The Politics*, c. 330 BC.

5 George Orwell, *England Your England*, 1941.

6 Edmund Burke, *Reflections on the Revolution in France*, 1790.

7 Georg Hegel, *Elements of the Philosophy of Right*, 1821.

8 Philip Gould, *The Unfinished Revolution: how the modernisers saved the Labour Party*, 1999.

9 Alexis de Tocqueville, *Democracy in America*, 1835-40.

10 Karl Polanyi, *On Liberalism and Liberty*, 1955.

11 Edmund Burke, *Reflections on the Revolution in France*, 1790.

12 George Orwell, *England Your England*, 1941.

1: Triangulation

1 Georg Hegel, *Elements of the Philosophy of Right*, 1821.

2 Thomas Hobbes, *Leviathan*, 1651.

3 Philip Gould, *The Unfinished Revolution: how the modernisers saved the Labour Party*, 1999.

4 Anthony Giddens, *The Third Way: the renewal of social democracy*, 1998.

2: Liberty and Equality

1 Edmund Burke, *Reflections on the Revolution in France*, 1790.

2 Immanuel Kant, *Groundwork of the Metaphysic of Morals*, 1785.

3 Roger Scruton, *The Meaning of Conservatism*, 1980.

4   David Hume, 'Of the Original Contract', *Essays Moral and Political*, 1741-42.

5   Georg Hegel, *Elements of the Philosophy of Right*, 1821.

6   John Stuart Mill, *On the Subjection of Women*, 1869.

7   Georg Hegel, *Elements of the Philosophy of Right*, 1821.

8   John Locke, *Second Treatise of Government*, 1690.

9   Thomas Hobbes, *Leviathan*, 1651.

10 Thomas Hobbes, *Leviathan*, 1651.

11 John Locke, *Second Treatise of Government*, 1690.

12 Adam Smith, *An Inquiry into the Nature and Causes of the Wealth of Nations*, 1776.

13 Hernando de Soto, *The Mystery of Capital: why capitalism triumphs in the west and fails everywhere else*, 2000.

14 Roger Scruton, *The Meaning of Conservatism*, 1980.

15 Aristotle, *The Politics*, c. 330.

16 Anthony Giddens, *The Third Way and its Critics*, 2000.

17 John Rawls, *A Theory of Justice*, 1971.

18 Edmund Burke, *An Appeal from the New to the Old Whigs*, 1791.

19 John Rawls, *A Theory of Justice*, 1971.

20 Thomas Hobbes, *Leviathan*, 1651.

21 Anthony Giddens, *The Third Way and its Critics*, 2000.

22 Anthony Crosland, *The Future of Socialism*, 1956.

23 Georg Hegel, *Elements of the Philosophy of Right*, 1821.

24 Anthony Giddens, *The Third Way: the renewal of social democracy*, 1998.

25 Robert Nozick, *Anarchy, State and Utopia*, 1974.

26 Friedrich von Hayek, *The Constitution of Liberty*, 1960.

27 Alexis de Tocqueville, *Democracy in America*, 1835-40.

28 Georg Hegel, *Elements of the Philosophy of Right*, 1821.

29 Anthony Giddens, *The Third Way: the renewal of social democracy*, 1998.

30 Plato, *The Republic*, c. 360.

3: Fraternity

1   Allan Cameron, introduction to Norberto Bobbio, *Left and Right: the significance of a political distinction*, 1997.

2   Georg Hegel, *Elements of the Philosophy of Right*, 1821.

3   Isaiah Berlin, *Two Concepts of Liberty*, 1958.

4   Georg Hegel, *Elements of the Philosophy of Right*, 1821.

5   Isaiah Berlin, *Two Concepts of Liberty*, 1958.

6   Georg Hegel, *Elements of the Philosophy of Right*, 1821.

7   George Eliot, *Middlemarch*, 1871.

8   Georg Hegel, *Elements of the Philosophy of Right*, 1821.

9   Roger Scruton, *On Hunting*, 1998.

10 Tony Blair, speech at the Old Vic Theatre, 17 June 2003.

11 Georg Hegel, *Elements of the Philosophy of Right*, 1821.

12 *St Paul's Letter to the Romans*, 13:10.

13 Jonathan Sacks, *The Dignity of Difference*, 2004.

14 Aristotle, *The Politics*, c. 330.

15 Roger Scruton, *England: an Elegy*, 2000.

16 *St Paul's First Letter to the Corinthians*, 10:23.

17 John Locke, *Second Treatise of Government*, 1690.

18 Thomas Hobbes, *Leviathan*, 1651.

19 John Stuart Mill, *On Liberty*, 1859.

20 William Shakespeare, *Troilus and Cressida*, Act I, Scene 3.

21 Friedrich von Hayek, *The Constitution of Liberty*, 1960.

22 John Stuart Mill, *On Liberty*, 1859.

23 Friedrich von Hayek, *The Constitution of Liberty*, 1960.

24 Michael Oakeshott, *Rationalism*, 1962.

25 Anthony Giddens, *The Third Way: the renewal of social democracy*, 1998.

26 George Orwell, *England Your England*, 1941.

27 Quoted in Simon Heffer, *Like the Roman: the life of Enoch Powell*, 1998.

28 Friedrich von Hayek, *The Constitution of Liberty*, 1960.

29 Georg Hegel, *Elements of the Philosophy of Right*, 1821.

30 Friedrich von Hayek, *The Constitution of Liberty*, 1960.

31 Anthony Giddens, *The Third Way and its Critics*, 1999.

32 Adam Smith, *An Inquiry into the Nature and Causes of the Wealth of Nations*, 1776.

33 Frederic Bastiat, *The Law*, 1850.

34 Alexis de Tocqueville, *Democracy in America*, 1835-40.

35 Benjamin Disraeli, *Sybil, or The Two Nations*, 1845.

36 Anthony Giddens, *The Third Way: the renewal of social democracy*, 1998.

37 John Paul II, *Memory and Identity: personal reflections*, 2005.

38 Georg Hegel, *Elements of the Philosophy of Right*, 1821.

39 Edmund Burke, *Reflections on the Revolution in France, 1790*; Hegel, *Elements of the Philosophy of Right*, 1821.

40 Thomas Hobbes, *Leviathan*, 1651.

41 Roger Scruton, *The Meaning of Conservatism*, 1980.

42 Ferdinand Mount, *The British Constitution Now*, 1992.

43 Edmund Burke, *Tracts Relating to the Popery Laws*, 1765.

44 Karl Popper, *The Open Society and Its Enemies*, 1945.

45 Friedrich von Hayek, *The Constitution of Liberty*, 1960.

46 Thomas Hobbes, *Leviathan*, 1651.

47 Georg Hegel, *Elements of the Philosophy of Right*, 1821.

Afterword

1 Edmund Burke, *An Appeal from the New to the Old Whigs*, 1791.

2 George Orwell, *England Your England*, 1941.

3 William Shakespeare, *Troilus and Cressida*, Act I Scene 3.

4 Edmund Burke, *Reflections on the Revolution in France*, 1790.